Bloom's
GUIDES

Harper Lee's
To Kill a Mockingbird

The Adventures of Huckleberry Finn

All the Pretty Horses

Animal Farm

The Autobiography of Malcolm X

The Awakening

The Bell Jar

Beloved

Beowulf

Black Boy

The Bluest Eye

Brave New World

The Canterbury Tales

Catch-22

The Catcher in the Rye

The Chosen

The Crucible

Cry, the Beloved Country

Death of a Salesman

Fahrenheit 451

A Farewell to Arms

Frankenstein

The Glass Menagerie

The Grapes of Wrath

Great Expectations

The Great Gatsby

Hamlet

The Handmaid's Tale

Heart of Darkness

The House on Mango Street

I Know Why the Caged Bird Sings

The Iliad

Invisible Man

Jane Eyre

The Joy Luck Club

The Kite Runner

Lord of the Flies

Macbeth

Maggie: A Girl of the Streets

The Member of the Wedding

The Metamorphosis

Native Son

Night

1984

The Odyssey

Oedipus Rex

Of Mice and Men

One Hundred Years of Solitude

Pride and Prejudice

Ragtime

A Raisin in the Sun

The Red Badge of Courage

Romeo and Juliet

The Scarlet Letter

A Separate Peace

Slaughterhouse-Five

Snow Falling on Cedars

The Stranger

A Streetcar Named Desire

The Sun Also Rises

A Tale of Two Cities

Their Eyes Were Watching God

The Things They Carried

To Kill a Mockingbird

Uncle Tom's Cabin

The Waste Land

Wuthering Heights

Bloom's
GUIDES

Harper Lee's
To Kill a Mockingbird
New Edition

Edited & with an Introduction
by Harold Bloom

BLOOM'S
LITERARY CRITICISM
An imprint of Infobase Publishing

Bloom's Guides: To Kill a Mockingbird—New Edition

Copyright © 2010 by Infobase Publishing

Introduction © 2010 by Harold Bloom

All rights reserved. No part of this book may be reproduced or utilized in any form or by any means, electronic or mechanical, including photocopying, recording, or by any information storage or retrieval systems, without permission in writing from the publisher. For information contact:

Bloom's Literary Criticism

An imprint of Infobase Publishing

132 West 31st Street

New York, NY 10001

Library of Congress Cataloging-in-Publication Data

Harper Lee's To kill a mockingbird / edited and with an introduction by Harold Bloom. — New ed.

   p. cm. — (Bloom's guides)

   Includes bibliographical references and index.

   ISBN 978-1-60413-811-5 (hardcover)

   1. Lee, Harper. To kill a mockingbird. 2. Race relations in literature. 3. Lawyers in literature. 4. Racism in literature. 5. Fathers and daughters in literature. 6. Girls in literature. I. Bloom, Harold.

   PS3562.E353T63355 2010

   813'.54—dc22

2009049160

Bloom's Literary Criticism books are available at special discounts when purchased in bulk quantities for businesses, associations, institutions, or sales promotions. Please call our Special Sales Department in New York at (212) 967–8800 or (800) 322–8755.

You can find Bloom's Literary Criticism on the World Wide Web at http://www.chelseahouse.com

Contributing editor: Portia Williams Weiskel

Cover designed by Takeshi Takahashi

Composition by IBT Global, Troy NY

Cover printed by Yurchak Printing, Landisville, Pa.

Book printed and bound by Yurchak Printing, Landisville, Pa.

Printed in the United States of America

All links and Web addresses were checked and verified to be correct at the time of publication. Because of the dynamic nature of the Web, some addresses and links may have changed since publication and may no longer be valid.

Contents

Introduction

The continued popularity of *To Kill a Mockingbird* (1960), a generation after its initial publication, raises, without answering, the crucial question about the novel. Is it only a period piece, charming but now outdated, or does it possess something of the stuff of permanence? It came out of our last Age of Innocence, the fifties, before the Vietnam War and the upheaval of the counterculture, and long before our current crises of race relations, economic dislocation, and the failure of faith in government, indeed in all authority. Rereading it returns one to an optimism about possibilities in human nature and in societal concern that many of us no longer share. Palpably, the book retains its pathos, but does it move us mostly through and by nostalgia? Is it now primarily a sentimental romance, touching but a shade childish, or is it, like J. D. Salinger's *The Catcher in the Rye*, another legitimate descendant of Mark Twain's *Adventures of Huckleberry Finn*, our classic romance of American childhood? Perhaps the questions can be summed up into one: Is Scout's narrative of her ninth year persuasively childlike, or is it essentially childish?

Jean Louise Finch, best known by her nickname, Scout, retains much of her charm as a classic American tomboy. She *is* indeed Harper Lee's book, being not only its narrator but much of its most interesting consciousness. Yet her deepest relation to Huck Finn, from whom she derives, is that, like him, she essentially cannot change. The crises of her book confirm her in her intrinsic strength and goodness, without wounding her sensibility or modifying her view of reality. Despite the villainous Ewell, and the conviction and death of the innocent Tom Robinson, a pure victim of Maycomb County racism, Scout retains not only her own idealism but her faith in the virtues of the people of her county. *To Kill a Mockingbird* comes out of an Alabama near related to William

Faulkner's Mississippi but in a cosmos apart from the world of *Light in August, As I Lay Dying, The Sound and the Fury*, and the other Faulknerian masterworks. Clearly it would be foolish to measure *To Kill a Mockingbird* against the best American novels of our past century, but is it wholly invalid to use Faulkner's vision of reality as a standard for reality testing in regard to Harper Lee's novel? Is her view of human nature adequate to a mature sense of the complexities of our existence? I myself am uncertain of the answers to these questions, but depending on which answers prove right, *To Kill a Mockingbird* will someday seem either a sentimental romance of a particular moment or a canonical narrative.

A formal critic could argue in favor of Harper Lee's aesthetic restraint, since how could we strictly expect traumatic change in so brief a span of time for a healthy nine-year-old girl? Yet the voice narrating the novel is that of the grown-up Jean Louise, studying the nostalgias of her ninth year and chronicling events clearly more remarkable than she has known since. Whatever life has brought her (and she tells us absolutely nothing about that), she evidently is fixated on what could be termed the era of Bob Ewell and of Boo Radley, would-be murderer and heroic savior, in her life and in the lives of Jem and of Atticus. That far-off era is a time warp, with a foreground but no afterground, from which we are excluded. And yet we can surmise that Boo Radley's heroic intervention was a decisive turning point for Scout, persuading her permanently of the benign resources inherent in even the most curtailed and wounded human nature.

To Kill a Mockingbird is an impossible book not to like; you can reject its idealisms, but the portrait of Scout Finch will linger on in you anyway. There are palpable formulaic elements in the book; even its largest surprises seem predictable enough. Still, the book is refreshingly free of ideologies and of the need to revise history to suit some particular politics of the spirit. The book's permanent importance, or lack thereof, turns on Scout's personality and character. She is neither Huck Finn battling for inner freedom while dreading solitude nor (in a lesser register) Holden Caulfield defending himself against breakdown and madness. Motherless, she yet has the best of fathers in Atticus and the best of brothers in Jem. Most of all, she has her self, a will-to-good so wholesome and open that it charms nearly everyone she encounters, short of the brutal Ewell and an officious relative or two. It is difficult to visualize a reader whom she will not charm, even at our time, in this place. Whether that charm will extend into days to come, I do not know.

Biographical Sketch

The youngest of four children, Nelle Harper Lee was born on April 28, 1926, to Frances Finch Cunningham Lee and Amasa Coleman Lee, a lawyer, in Monroeville, Alabama. One of Lee's childhood friends was Truman Capote, who would also become a celebrated novelist and essayist. She graduated from high school in Monroeville and then attended Huntingdon College, a private school for women in Montgomery, for a year (1944–45) before transferring to the University of Alabama. In 1947, she enrolled in the university's law school, later spending a year as an exchange student at Oxford University. She withdrew, however, in 1949, six months before she would have received a law degree and moved to New York City to pursue a writing career.

Lee had begun writing at the age of seven, and she had also written a variety of satires, reviews, and columns during her years in college. In New York, while working as an airline reservations clerk, she wrote several essays and short stories; none of these was published, but an agent encouraged her to expand one of the stories into a novel.

Receiving financial support from friends, Lee gave up her job and worked on the novel *To Kill a Mockingbird*, which was a fictionalized account of the Scottsboro Trial and would be her only book. Although she spent much time shuttling between New York and Monroeville tending to her ailing father, she finished a draft of the novel in 1957. An editor at the publishing firm J. B. Lippincott, Tay Hohoff, suggested revisions, and Lee rewrote the book. It was published in 1960.

To Kill a Mockingbird was an instant popular success, even though early reviews were mixed: Some critics found the work too moralistic, while others found the narrative of Scout's girlhood to be corrupted by her adult sensibilities. A year after its publication, the novel had sold 500,000 copies and had been translated into ten languages. By 1982, more than 15,000,000 copies had been sold, and the book remains popular among students and the general public. It won a number of awards, including the Pulitzer Prize, the Alabama Library Association Award, and the Brotherhood Award of the National Conference of Christians and Jews. In 1962, it was adapted into a major motion picture in which Gregory Peck played the role of Atticus Finch. Lee was offered the chance to write the screenplay, but she declined; it was written by Horton Foote. The film won four Academy Awards, including Best Actor (Peck) and Best Adaped Screenplay (Foote). In 1970, Christopher Sergel's dramatic adaptation of *To Kill a Mockingbird* was published, and it has been performed widely throughout the United States and England.

Harper Lee has been guarded about her private life and about the sources for *To Kill a Mockingbird*. She has also written—or, at least, published—very little since the appearance of her novel, aside from a few pieces in magazines and a foreword written for the 35th anniversary edition of *To Kill a Mockingbird*. She gave considerable assistance to her boyhood friend Truman Capote in the research for his "nonfiction novel" *In Cold Blood* (1964), which is dedicated to Lee and Jack Dunphy. In June 1966, Harper Lee was one of two persons named by President Johnson to the National Council of Arts. She has been awarded a number of honorary degrees, including a doctorate from the University of Alabama in 1990 and one from Spring Hill College in Mobile, Alabama, in 1997. She continues to reside in Monroeville, Alabama.

The Story Behind the Story

To Kill a Mockingbird is set in the early 1930s during the Great Depression in the rural southern town of Maycomb, Alabama. Despite Harper Lee's insistence that *To Kill a Mockingbird* is a work of fiction, certain places and characters bear a remarkable resemblance to those in Monroeville, Alabama, her hometown. Lee was born in 1926, which would make her exactly Scout's age ("almost six") at the start of the novel. Those who grew up in Lee's hometown remember one family's house, the Boulars, which was "boarded up and falling down," directly across the street from the Lee home and the mysterious denizen named Sonny Boular who almost certainly became the model for Boo Radley. Lee's father, Amasa Lee, was also a lawyer like Atticus Finch. It is therefore almost impossible to separate the novel, and most importantly, the precocious, tomboy character of Scout, from the author and her life.

Little is known about the life of Harper Lee. She is famously reclusive, divides her time between New York City and Monroeville, and is rumored to be working on her second novel. She was born Nelle Harper Lee, the youngest of four children, to Frances Finch Cunningham Lee and Amasa Coleman Lee. She attended law school in Montgomery but never finished; she also spent a year at Oxford and worked behind the reservations desk at an airline. Since the publication of *To Kill a Mockingbird*, which took her eight years to write, the body of her published work has been limited to a few published essays in magazines. As far as her character is concerned, a glimpse of wryness is discernable in a handful of interviews conducted in the publicity frenzy surrounding the novel's 1960 publication, its 1961 Pulitzer Prize, and the subsequent 1962 film. For example, when asked, "Is it true your sister is a criminal lawyer?" Lee responded, "She's not a criminal, no."

The most vivid depiction of Lee that exists, however, is through the recollections of her childhood friend, Truman Capote. Capote, who transforms Lee into the slightly terrifying tomboy Idabel in his first novel, *Other Voices, Other Rooms*, is himself immortalized as Dill in *Mockingbird*. Most biographers agree that no apter description of him as a boy exists than the one Lee conjures. Dill/Capote is a boy of almost psychotic imagination; a prophetic liar who is constantly inventing stories, many of them to explain his absent mother and father, in short:

> a curiosity. He wore blue linen shorts that buttoned to his shirt, his hair was snow white and stuck to his head like duckfluff; he was a year my senior but I towered over him . . . a pocket Merlin whose head teemed with eccentric plans, strange longings, and quaint fancies.

Capote, in turn, remembers Lee as a girl who bullied boys, including him. Lee's mother was an eccentric and a gossip who also tried to drown her in the bath at least twice. While Capote found himself in trouble at the age of eleven when he published "Mrs. Busybody" in the local paper, perhaps Lee also borrowed elements from her mother to help create *Mockingbird*'s local gossip Miss Stephanie. Lee and Capote were the best of friends, an effeminate, undersized boy and an aggressive girl, both of them outcasts of their youth, sharing a precocious love of reading and a fascination with the goings on in Monroeville. Lee was a girl determined to have her own way. Moreover, when Capote set out for Kansas to report on the murders that formed the centerpiece of his book in *In Cold Blood*, it was Lee who accompanied him. It was also Lee—tireless, garrulous, and accustomed to farm folk and their ways—who ultimately unlocked the tightly sealed lips of the residents of the small midwestern town. Apparently, Dill and Scout had not outgrown their morbid fancies. It is reassuring to think that young Lee was probably just as stubborn as her doppelganger Scout, and that Scout the adult would maintain her liveliness.

Historical Background
On March 25, 1931, nine black men were arrested in Scottsboro, Alabama, accused of raping two white women on a train. The Scottsboro trials have become notorious, especially in civil rights

history. The women, Victoria Price and Ruby Bates, were mill-town residents of dubious virtue, and it became increasingly apparent, especially after Bates withdrew her charges, that they leveled the accusation of rape to avoid being arrested for vagrancy. (They, and their two male companions, who were also their lovers, had stowed away on the train.) As is explained in *Mockingbird*, rape in 1930s Alabama was a capital crime and all defendants faced the death penalty. There was an overwhelming lack of physical evidence—Price, who had said that she was knocked on the head with a gun, beaten repeatedly, and raped by the nine men on a bed of spiky concrete, sported several small bruises on her backside, which, as the defending attorney and also the judge pointed out, could be caused by traveling, as the women did, in a coal carrier.

Nevertheless, all nine men were convicted, followed by a flurry of appeals that would continue, until 1973, when one of the defendants, Clarence Norris, who had been on death row, was pardoned. There are numerous parallels to the trial of Tom Robinson in *To Kill a Mockingbird*, not solely in the blatantly unfair verdict rendered because of prejudice. There is also the issue of debilitation. One of the accused men in the Scottsboro trial was physically impaired, the other practically blind, and just as it was virtually impossible for Tom to have beaten Mayella with his withered left hand, it was also as impossible for these two men to have crossed the train yard and found their way to the coal car that Price alleged was the scene of the crime. The dogged defense attorney Samuel Liebowitz also echoes the noble Atticus in his determination to acquit the nine men. Atticus, as well as the fictional Judge Taylor, are most indebted to the judge that presided over the Scottsboro trials, James E. Horton. Horton was virtuous, not unlike Judge Taylor, who, as Miss Maudie wisely points out, appointed Atticus particularly for the case. Or in her words, "Did it ever strike you that Judge Taylor naming Atticus to defend that boy was no accident?" Horton famously "put aside" a guilty verdict and hence ensured that he would not be voted in as judge the following year. Like Atticus, he outlines the overwhelming lack of evidence, though Atticus's ultimate condemnation of Mayella Ewell:

I say guilt, gentlemen, because it was guilt that motivated her . . . she struck out at her victim—of necessity, she must put him away from her—he must be removed from her presence, and from the world.

is considerably softer than Horton's closing remarks:

History, sacred and profane, and the common experience of mankind teach us that women of the character shown in this case are prone for selfish reasons to make false accusations of both rape and insult upon the slightest provocation, or even without provocation for ulterior purposes.

Similarities certainly exist between the real and fictitious judges.

We also have to remember that *To Kill a Mockingbird* was completed in 1960 and published in New York. Perhaps some of the reason for its immediate popularity is due to the fact that it was not written in 1930s Alabama, whose unjust climate provides the story's fuel, but rather that it was written at the height of the civil rights movement. Five years before its publication, Rosa Parks refused to give up her seat on a bus in Montgomery, Alabama. Martin Luther King Jr., who was already at the forefront of the movement, led the subsequent Montgomery bus boycott and his house was bombed. It had been three years since the court-ordered desegregation of schools in Little Rock, Arkansas. In 1960, tangible change was evident; *Mockingbird*, written during this unstable time, looks back to an era when there was relative calm. Some critics have argued *To Kill a Mockingbird* may not be *that* radical of a book, because Harper Lee is critical of the past but does not draw attention to the turbulence of the civil rights movement. The novel was banned in some parts of the country, primarily due to its references of rape and use of the word *nigger* but otherwise drew accolades for its sympathetic portrayal of black characters. Lee was allowed to continue her life in Monroeville—the town that *Mockingbird* condemns for its closed-mindedness—in peace.

List of Characters

Known best by her nickname **Scout**, which implies a character of honest, indomitable curiosity, Jean Louise Finch remains one of the most endearing of child narrators and is generally assumed to be her creator's doppelganger. She is nearly six when the novel begins and almost nine when it ends. A tomboy, her mother dies when she is two; she has no female friends to speak of and regards the women of the town who are supposed to be her exemplars with a mixture of fear and awe. Scout distinguishes herself most prominently through her ferocious temperament and her inability to keep her thoughts to herself.

From the outset, we know that **Jeremy "Jem" Finch** will be his father's son—a future lawyer and gentleman who will carry on Atticus's legacy. A loner, he has a gentler personality than his firebrand sister, and yet his temper, when finally sparked, is a violent one nonetheless; he vandalizes Mrs. Dubose's camellias when she taunts his father. Scout's elder by four years, the novel recounts Jem Finch's passage to adulthood.

A widower, attorney, and father of two in his fifties, **Atticus Finch** is the undisputed hero of the book—the moral force of both the story and the town and the quintessence of a southern gentleman. Even Atticus's strengths are nonetheless called into question when he is asked to defend Tom Robinson, a black man accused of raping a white girl.

Dill Harris first distinguishes himself by his diminutive size; he is more than a year older than Scout, but she towers over him. He is also a consummate liar, highly sensitive, physically unprepossessing, and comforts himself about his broken family by telling fantastic stories about his father. He spends the three summers with his aunt who lives in the Finch's neighborhood. It is general knowledge that he is modeled on Lee's childhood friend Truman Capote. Perhaps there is no more revealing moment than when Dill announces that he wants, when he grows older, to be a "clown."

Calpurnia or **"Cal"** is the most complicated and successful African-American character in the book. As the Finches' cook, she is as close to a mother as either Jem or Scout has ever known, except that she is harsher than a mother, while in many ways more idealistic. She is not a gentle woman, but as Atticus says, "She's tried to bring them [the children] according to her lights, and Cal's lights are pretty good." She is also, perhaps, an example of the potential for the African-American community—as one of its only members who can read and write. Though she recognizes her inferior position as a cook, Calpurnia rarely neglects to speak her mind.

Arthur "Boo" Radley is the shadow, the bogeyman, of the book. Boo only reveals himself at the end, though his presence provides much fodder for the children's imagination. It is rumored that he stabbed his father in the leg with scissors, and since that episode, he has never set foot outside the Radley house. Nevertheless, he leaves the children presents in the hollow of a tree and saves their lives—proving his humanity and decency before vanishing for good behind the Radley threshhold.

A widow, **Maudie Atkinson** grows azaleas and bakes the best cakes in town, while also providing guidance to the children. Her character is a blend of shrewdness, humor, and compassion. It is typical of Miss Maudie to comment, as her house burns down, that she always wanted a smaller house anyway because it would give her a larger garden. Together with Atticus, she is the closest thing to the town's conscience.

Tom Robinson is the central victim of the story. A strong black man, he also has a shriveled left hand, which proves that he was unable to commit the crime of which he is accused—that of beating and raping Mayella Ewell—as the marks on her body indicate a left-handed perpetrator. He is condemned nonetheless and then shot seventeen times when he attempts to escape.

Just as Atticus is the hero and Tom is the victim, so **Robert "Bob" Ewell** is the villain. Unnuanced in his portrayal, Ewell is a drunken, lazy man, representative of pure evil. A left-handed man, the evidence points that it was he who beat his daughter and possibly raped her as well. ("She says she never kissed a growed man before . . ." Tom reports about Mayella, "She says what her daddy do to her don't count.") Ewell later tries to kill the Finch children and is stabbed by Boo Radley in the attempt.

The epitome of southern graciousness and hospitality, **Aunt Alexandra** is Atticus's older sister who stays with the Finch family the summer of the trial. Though Scout initially resents Aunt Alexandra's attempts to turn her into a little lady, she ultimately respects Aunt Alexandra for defending Atticus's character.

Mayella Ewell is Bob Ewell's daughter who accuses Tom Robinson of rape, even though it is clear that her father has abused her.

Heck Tate is the upstanding sheriff of Maycomb who always tries to do right by the citizens. He is also a witness at Tom's trial.

The son of a poor farmer, **Walter Cunningham** is one of Scout's classmates whom the Finch family invites to dinner.

Mr. Walter Cunningham is a poor but decent farmer who initially is part of the mob that wants to kill Tom. He changes his mind at the persistence of Scout.

Mrs. Henry Lafayette Dubose is a cantankerous older woman who lives near the Finches. Though she angers Jem by insulting his father, he learns that Atticus respects her because she is honest and courageous in battling a morphine addiction.

Summary and Analysis

To Kill a Mockingbird consists of two parts and three distinct sections connected by devices that are sometimes successful and sometimes haphazard. Part 1 includes chapters 1 through 11 and is arguably the most powerful and coherent section of the book. The second section, which includes chapters 12–25, details Tom Robinson's trial and subsequent death. The third section, also in part 2, is a quick effort to draw all the elements of the plot together, and happily so. It details Maycomb after Tom's death and the aftermath of the trial. Most importantly, it describes how Scout and Jem are attacked by Bob Ewell on their way home from their school pageant.

The first section of the book (**chapters 1–11**) is primarily about southern childhood, but it heavily foreshadows the events in parts 2 and 3—the small dramas in part 1 will be magnified later at Tom's trial. Scout opens by explaining, "When he was nearly thirteen, my brother Jem got his arm badly broken at the elbow"—the point to which the book will eventually return, so that we are not taken in by the initial, contented, almost lazy pace.

A hodgepodge of characters is introduced, each with his or her own manner of speaking and odd traits. Among the adults alone these include bespectacled Atticus; dotty Miss Maudie; chatterbox Miss Stephanie; hearty Heck Tate; domineering Calpurnia who taught her son—the local garbage collector—to read from Blackstone's *Commentaries*; and sour Mr. Avery, whose hobby is to whittle stockwood into toothpicks. Also introduced is Maycomb, so vivid with personality that it is almost a character in itself. Maycomb is a "tired old town" where doors are never locked and everyone knows one another's business. It is also implied that Maycomb has a mildly incestuous reputation; out in the neighborhood of Old Sarum, "the Cunninghams married the Coninghams until the spelling of the names was academic—academic until a Cunningham disputed a Coningham over land titles and took to the law."

Similarly, among gentlefolk, Atticus is "related by blood or marriage to nearly every family in the town."

The first few pages of *To Kill a Mockingbird* contain some of its most descriptive writing:

> In rainy weather the streets turned to red slop, grass grew on sidewalks, the courthouse sagged in the square. Somehow it was hotter then . . . Men's collars wilted by nine in the morning. Ladies bathed before noon, after their three o'clock naps, and by nightfall were like soft teacakes with frostings of sweat and sweet talcum.

This is a child's imaginative vision recalled with adult grace. Though Scout's perspective is never corrupted, Lee does not condescend by making her sound infantile.

Scout and Jem are the only children of the town lawyer, Atticus Finch. Atticus is middle-aged and a widower, and his children are often paranoid about their father's apparent lack of a traditional male persona. He does not hunt like the other men in town, nor does he "play poker, fish, drink or smoke." He has never remarried, which sparks taunts from vindictive townspeople like Mrs. Henry Lafayette Dubose, nor has he ever physically punished his children. From the beginning, the reader is aware that Atticus is heroic, but he is far from redeeming himself as a hero in his children's eyes. "Atticus," Scout tells us, "was feeble: he was nearly fifty," and he didn't "do anything that could possibly arouse the admiration of anyone." Far more authoritative, at least in Scout's eyes, is the Finches' black cook, Calpurnia, who reads, forces Scout to practice penmanship, and also slaps her at will. Yet the children are terrified of Atticus's judgment, without knowing exactly why. Or in Jem's words, "Atticus ain't ever whipped me as far as I can remember. I wanna keep it that way."

Dill Harris arrives in Maycomb to spend the summer with his aunt, and he quickly reveals a natural ability to tell lies; he and the Finch children become fast friends. For approximately the first fifty pages of the novel, the reader is shown how idyllic life in Maycomb can be. Certainly small-mindedness exists, and while Maycomb is an old town, its courage is placed in question as being one of the only towns left undamaged by the Civil War. It is the height of the Depression, and everyone is poor; yet in this enclosed, impoverished, sweltering world, children can roam and play. Doors are always open, and neighbors pay social calls every Sunday. "People," Lee explains, "moved slowly then," and such a pace gives the young room to invent games, run rampant on the town streets, and stay safe.

Jem and Scout's first summer with Dill is delightful, especially because there is nothing that can make a child's paradise more complete than a mystery. Maycomb citizen Boo Radley is that mystery. He lives in the boarded-up "droopy and sick" house and never comes out, is rumored to have stabbed his father with a pair of scissors, and scatters, poisoned pecans in his yard. The children incorporate the mystery of Boo Radley into their games; they dare each other to touch Boo's front door, try to write him letters, and devise their own mini-plays that they perform on the street. While children may be enchanting creatures, Lee is firm in her conviction that they are not wholly innocent. They would be bored, after all, with swapping comics and reenacting King Kong and Tom Swift. Danger adds an element of unpredictability to their lives.

Scout's first day of school marks the start of action in what has been so far a somewhat indolent book. Scout is not emotionally equipped to deal with the tribulations of everyday life, as the action in the classroom demonstrates. She is humiliated by the teacher because she can already read—she is bored—and then, as a final blow, she is rapped on the knuckles with a ruler. These schoolroom scenes contain some of the most endearing moments in the book: the naive teacher, Miss Caroline, who insists on the "Dewey Decimal" system of education and faints at the sight of cooties; and the overgrown kids who have repeated the first grade already three times. Miss Caroline reading this raggedy bunch of children a story about cats in "cunning little clothes" is almost as entertaining as the vision of her waving cards printed with words like *cat, rat, man,* and *you.* " . . . [T]he class," Scout explains, "received these impressionistic revelations in silence."

All the white children in Maycomb attend the same school, and children of sharecroppers and the lowliest residents share blackboards with the children of lawyers, which was standard practice in 1930s Alabama. Camille Maxwell Elebash remembers, "I always took two lunches, one for myself, one for someone else." (Johnson, 147) At the age of six, Scout is faced with the challenge of fitting in, and it is not a prospect that she relishes. In addition, Walter Cunningham, the son of a poor farmer, is invited to dinner with the Finch family and pours syrup over his entire supper. Later, Calpurnia slaps Scout (who has brought this table manner to loud attention), for Walter, despite his hookworms and bare feet, is decent enough to be the Finches' "comp'ny"; though his father is poor, he is different from many of the dubious characters that share his economic bracket. Mr. Cunningham never has the money to pay for services, but he will repay in potatoes and stockwood. His family is honest and hardworking, if uneducated and impoverished, and they deserve to be treated with respect. The only other significant episode during the school year is that Boo Radley has started leaving the children presents in the oak tree—pieces of gum, Indian head pennies, a broken gold watch.

The following summer, Scout establishes a friendship with their neighbor Miss Maudie Atkinson, who, despite her eccentricity, is proud and well-bred in her own way, meriting people's respect; together with Atticus and Calpurnia, she establishes herself as another mouthpiece for right. Later, Dill, Jem, and Scout try to break into the Radley house. In the shooting that follows, Jem loses his trousers on the barbed wire fence, and when he returns in the middle of the night to retrieve them, finds them stitched and folded neatly over the fence.

The next winter, snow falls, significant because it is a strange occurrence for Maycomb and a foreshadowing of events to come. Jem makes a snowman out of mud and piles snow on top, essentially a "nigger snowman" that he has whitened, but symbolic because it signifies how shallow the divisions of color actually are. Furthermore, he first makes the snowman into a caricature of their neighbor Mr. Avery, and then, at Atticus's suggestion, adds Miss Maudie's hat. Whether the snowman is now a woman or a man becomes ambiguous. That night, the coldest night in Maycomb, opposites coincide once again as Miss Maudie's house catches fire and, despite the snow, flames consume her precious azaleas. Unnoticed, Boo Radley slips outside and covers the shivering Scout with a blanket.

For Christmas, Jem and Scout are given air rifles. In perhaps what is the most obviously significant exchange in the first section (conversational exchanges will increase after chapter 12) Atticus tells them that "it's a sin to kill a mockingbird."

The action moves to February, when Atticus shoulders a rifle and kills a mad dog in one shot. It is a deeply pregnant moment, emphasized by the still trees and the silenced mockingbirds, and Atticus's emasculating spectacles falling to the ground and breaking. For the first time in Maycomb, the doors are closed tightly. Only Calpurnia has latched and then unlatched the screen door in anticipation. Just as he will do for Tom Robinson, Atticus stands alone in confronting madness for the sake of the town, a threat made all the more menacing because it is quiet. In Scout's words, "I thought that mad dogs foamed at the mouth, galloped, leaped, and lunged at throats . . . Had [the dog] behaved thus, I would have been less frightened." Yet despite its leaden symbolism, this episode is redeemed by the children's response. They had no idea, up until this point, Atticus could even wield a gun, and he is now a hero in their eyes. Before he can prove his virility to them by virtue in the courtroom, he first must prove it on a physical level.

In another episode, Jem tears down Mrs. Henry Lafayette Dubose's precious camellias, his response when she insults his father, "Your father's no better than the niggers and trash that he works for!" First Miss Maudie's azaleas are ruined, and then Mrs. Dubose's snow-on-the-mountains. Everywhere flowers—a symbol of everything feminine and genteel in the South—are being destroyed. There is no more fitting symbol of landed southern womanhood, of course, than the camellia, and in ravaging Mrs. Dubose's bushes, Jem, essentially, is attacking her heritage and her pride. Jem's penance, enforced rather mysteriously by Atticus, is to read to her from *Ivanhoe* every Sunday. In the end, Mrs. Dubose dies, and Atticus reveals that the weekly reading was the way that Mrs. Dubose had weaned herself from a morphine addiction. She leaves Jem a camellia, a symbol that her old South will endure despite how he might try to angrily knock it down; and even after her death we are left perplexed as to why Atticus defends her and refuses to let his enraged son throw the blossom upon the fire. Hovering, of course, over these later episodes is the one momentous event that will propel the story from being an ordinary catalogue of quirky day-to-day events into high drama. Atticus has been appointed to defend a black man, Tom Robinson, who has been charged with raping a white girl, Mayella Ewell.

If there is one consistency in the novel, it is that the children, throughout, are learning to distinguish between hearsay and the truth. As Atticus claims, "I just hope that Jem and Scout come to me for their answers instead of listening to the town." However, it is interesting that the children first find out about the case through gossip. Atticus, noble man that he is, sometimes behaves in perplexing ways. He allows Scout to overhear his conversation with Uncle Jack, but he rarely confronts his children about the issue—or, indeed, any issue. This is Atticus's way; the children have to ask him first. Perhaps this is why the children are not aware of the magnitude of the things to come at the end of part 1. Perhaps this is also why Scout emerges at the end of the book relatively unscathed. Jem and Dill, older and far more deeply sensitive, will be wounded. But Scout lacks the understanding to be truly hurt by what happens—and no one gives it to her. Though three years older than at the beginning of the novel, she emerges from the story with the innocence still typical of a nine-year-old. What matters most is defending her honor—which is still wounded quickly but never permanently—and surviving school.

The events of section 2 (**chapters 12–25**) are less episodic and more melodramatically charged. By the time Calpurnia takes Jem and Scout to the local black church, Tom Robinson's trial is imminent. Here, Scout learns that everyone with the exception of four members of the black community—including

Cal and her son, Zeebo—is illiterate, a shock to someone for whom reading was so natural that it never occurred to her how she may have learned it, since Cal was instrumental in teaching Scout to write. In the short time leading up to the trial, Scout learns a great deal about race relations.

Several events occur that propel the action in the pivotal second section of the novel. Dill returns to Maycomb—he has left Mississippi and his unfeeling parents. In a small, yet poignant moment, Scout realizes what it might feel like to be unloved. Lack of love is not just being chained in the basement, as Dill first claims his mother and stepfather have done: " . . . they do get along better without me, I can't help them any. They ain't mean. . . . They kiss you and hug you good night and good mornin' and good bye and tell you they love you." Dill feels Maycomb is the only place where he is valued. Scout, on the other hand, is always needed in a way that she has just begun to understand.

Also at this point in the novel Aunt Alexandra suddenly takes command of the household. Alexandra, who in Scout's recollections often resembled a battleship and gave her an "add-a-pearl necklace," is not a welcome addition to Scout's life with her ideas that little girls should play with tea sets. Scout can feel the walls of a "pink cotton penitentiary" closing in. Curiously enough, Atticus does not object to her presence—in fact, he does not even inform the children that she is coming. In his mystifying way, he explains that Scout must obey her, must obey him, and must obey Calpurnia, even though the three perspectives rarely coincide. It is as if seven-year-old Scout is thrust into a perpetual contradiction. But Atticus, in the end, is always right. Ultimately, Alexandra's behavior upon hearing of Tom's death will be a study of majesty, and will make Scout realize that the true southern lady is not simply artifice.

The trial of Tom Robinson is famous. Whether or not it accurately represents the judicial proceedings in southern small towns at the time is not certain—from the hysterics of the witnesses and a judge who calls both attorneys by their first names and looks as though he is about to fall asleep when he is not munching his cigar (he does not light it but consumes it to its tip and then spits the whole mess out), to Atticus's lengthy and powerful conclusion. It is, however, one of the purest and most perfect examples of a mistrial. Not only is there no existing medical evidence to support that Mayella Ewell has actually been raped, but Mayella has bruises that could only have been inflicted by someone left-handed. Her father is left-handed, and it becomes increasingly apparent that Mayella is a victim of her father's sexual advances. The blatant injustice of the trial, coupled with Lee's great character sketches, is a testament to her superior storytelling abilities.

In many ways, the pretrial is more sordid than the deliberate miscarriage of justice that follows. The families—both black and white—picnic on fried chicken, sardines, and cola around the courthouse; this trial to them is a fête, as it is the most exciting thing to happen in Maycomb in years. But the reason this scene is so powerful is because the reader witnesses it through Scout's eyes, with a child's sense of anticipation and eagerness of this "gala occasion," even though to an adult with a sense of moral decency it is quite appalling. "It's like a Roman carnival," sneers Miss Maudie, who declines to attend. Thus the dichotomy between the childhood fantasy world of Scout and the actual events of the trial demonstrates the ugliness of the situation.

Right before the trial commences, an incident occurs in which Scout disperses an angry mob that has assembled at the county jail to lynch Tom. In this scene, Atticus is standing guard over Tom Robinson's cell, and just as the children happen upon him, the men approach. For a while, violence seems inevitable as the mob grows more impatient. Then, Scout singles out Mr. Cunningham—tenant farmer, client of Atticus, and father of her aforementioned schoolmate Walter—from the crowd and questions him about Walter. Failing that, she pursues the topic of entailments.

Atticus had said that it was polite to talk to people about what they were interested in, not what about you were interested in. Mr. Cunningham displayed no interest in his son, so I tackled his entailment as a last ditch effort to make him feel at home.

Just minutes before, Scout has kicked the man who has laid a hand on her brother. "Barefoot," she explains, "I was surprised to see him fall back in real pain. I intended to kick his shin, but aimed too high." Moments like this lighten the tense scene. W. J. Stuckey, who dismissed *Mockingbird* as "self-consciously cute" points out the scene's key faults. Its climax, Stuckey states, revolves around Mr. Cunningham doing "a particular thing"— "these are rhetorical tricks resorted to by fiction writers when they are unable to cope with the difficult problem of rendering a scene dramatically. The author wants Mr. Cunningham to have a change of heart . . . but she is unable to bring it off . . ." (Stuckey, 194). Furthermore, Stuckey notes that Mr. Cunningham has not, until then, been distinguished as a leader in any way, so the act of him calling off the mob with the wave of the hand is somewhat dubious. Dramatically, the scene is flawed; yet it sparks a reaction in the reader. Despite the fact that Stuckey might call Scout accidentally kicking an aggressor an example of Lee's "cuteness," it is a poignant moment in the scene. Atticus sums up why Scout and Finch have rescued him that night: "You children last night made Walter Cunningham stand in my shoes for a minute." If they did, it was through laughter and lightness. The humor of youth not only saves Atticus, and temporarily Tom, it also saves the scene itself, for the dearest moments of *Mockingbird* are those that make us chuckle. "Laughter," Lee explains, about an earlier confrontation between Atticus and the gentlefolk, "broke them up." Scout's humor, which springs from her mulish, pared-down notions, is arguably the most skilled element in the book. Lee manages to make Scout's humor seem effortless, which lifts a moral melodrama above mawkishness.

The trial encompasses **chapters 16–20**, of which Tom's powerful testimony is considered to be the book's climax; both succinct and colorful, in many ways it is almost too humble and credible. He not only describes what happened on November 21—the day of the alleged rape—but also provides pivotal information about Mayella Ewell. "She says she never kissed a grown man before an' she might as well kiss a nigger," Tom says, "She says what her papa do to her doesn't count." Even

27

though Tom Robinson's testimony is near perfect, certain factors compromise this scene. First, the book has transformed from childhood nostalgia story to "morality play;" critic R. A. Dave, who has nothing but praise for the book, says that the courtroom narrative "is in the danger of getting lost in the doldrums of discussion—dull, heavy, futile." (Dave, 56)

To Kill a Mockingbird is not a consistent book. As Granville Hicks points out, it "is not primarily about the childhood experience," for Lee has the bigger issue of "the perennial southern problem" on her mind. Her challenge, in Hicks's mind, "has been to tell the story she wants to tell and stay within the consciousness of a child." (Bloom, 5) There is not one story in *To Kill a Mockingbird*, but several, and the principal plot line is one that is too morally weighty for a child of nine to comprehend. Hence, in an effort not to compromise Scout's childlike perspective, Lee has put the rather weighty aspects of her tale into the mouths of her adults. The adults, therefore, in part 2, become noticeably less endearing. In part 1, Atticus is certainly already an idealist, yet he is also a wry widower engaged in the honest struggle of raising two children on his own. In part 2, he is a mouthpiece for justice. Surely there is nothing more disappointing than the batty, yet unquestionably elegant Miss Maudie launching into a speech:

> The handful of people who say that fair judgement is not marked White Only; the handful of people who say a fair trial is for everybody, not just us; the handful of people with enough humility to think, when they look at a Negro, there but for the Lordkindness am I.

Granted, Miss Maudie, like Atticus, has shared her wisdom throughout the novel, but it has been within her character—slightly obscure in meaning and always dry. This speech is not conversation, but a sermon.

There is not much that is artless about *To Kill a Mockingbird*. Actions are deliberate—Atticus shooting the rabid dog, Calpurnia taking the children to the black church. Only the children, especially Scout, are really natural in this symbol-laden world, and their naturalness is never better expressed than it is with Scout's wondering voice.

If we are devastated by Tom's fate, therefore, it is because earlier we have laughed at characters and their actions that may have played a role in it. The warmth that permeates the book, that even frames Tom's trial—before with Miss Maudie calling after Miss Stephanie, "Better be careful he doesn't hand you a subpoena" and immediately after with the grinning Atticus threatening to eat pickled pork knuckles in the dining room underneath his prim sister's nose—is turned on its head.

There is even slapstick during the trial itself. When the prosecuting attorney objects that the defense is "browbeating" the witness, the judge snorts, "Oh sit down, Horace, he's doing nothing of the sort. If anything, the witness is browbeating Atticus." In this instance, however, the only person to laugh is the judge. The rest of the courtroom is so silent that Scout wonders whether the babies have been "smothered at their mother's breast." This is the same sort of silence that greeted Atticus upon shooting the wild dog. Such a cessation of laughter is chilling, for what we have accepted as humorous is amusing no longer. Though the judge cracks jokes, doors are left unlocked, and children are allowed to ramble free at all hours of the night, intimacy comes with a price—narrow-mindedness. Suddenly, small town generosity curdles as quaint Maycomb habits reveal their menace, and one realizes that the price of little freedoms is suffocation on a grand scale. Those who sense it most acutely, it appears, are the most innocent members—the infants.

The trial is the one event of the book when we get little sense of Scout's thought process. Her role in the trial episode is as reporter; somehow her young mind is able to recall everything that was done and said. This is an adult arena, and she provides little commentary, except when Atticus loosens his clothing to prepare for his final address: " . . . he unbuttoned his vest, unbuttoned his collar, loosened his tie and took off his coat . . . to Jem and me, this was the equivalent of him standing before us stark naked." Such a comment is made only to underscore the symbolic significance of this gesture. Atticus is like a gladiator or a boxer stripping before a fight, or even more so, like a sacrifice in preparation to be slaughtered for the common good.

Jem and Dill feel the trial's pain most acutely; in many ways Scout is too young to comprehend the gravity of the situation. As Jem tells Reverend Sykes, "I think it's okay, Reverend, she doesn't understand it." It is telling that of the three children, Scout alone does not shed tears. Dill runs out during the prosecution's cross-examination—treating a human being with such a lack of respect makes the sensitive boy sick. Jem cries later that night. But it is precisely because the rest of the trial is so fun for them that its conclusion is devastating—they sneak away and break the rules to attend; they sit upstairs with Reverend Sykes and the rest of the black townspeople, which is the greatest adventure of all. The scene in which the children await the verdict is well orchestrated. The children are truly heady with excitement; not only have they attended the most important event in Maycomb history, they have also been caught and have gotten away with it. Despite Calpurnia's protests, Atticus lets them return to the courtroom after supper. "I was exhilarated," Scout recounts, "So many things had happened so fast I felt it would take years to sort them out . . . what new marvels would the evening bring?" No one stops to wonder whether it is right to feel so giddy when a man's life is at stake. Such giddiness behooves youth alone.

Ultimately, it will be Jem who is cut the deepest by the trial's conclusion, for he is the oldest. When he burbles, "We've won, haven't we?" he is only setting himself up for heartbreak. When Tom is pronounced guilty, Scout is dizzy; but Jem, who remains hyperconscious, weeps through the night and cannot eat the next morning. Scout's daze is engendered from her lack of understanding and the fact that she has, just minutes before, woken up from a nap on the Reverend Sykes's shoulder. Jem, on the other hand, finds himself confronted for the first time with the wrongs of the world. He is just sophisticated enough to grasp hatred in its fullest implications and is too vulnerable not to be shaken. As he says to Scout later, "I think I'm beginning to understand why Boo Radley's stayed shut up in the house all this time . . . it's because he *wants* to stay inside."

Dramatically, the most accomplished and certainly subtlest episode in part 3 is the Missionary Ladies Society's tea party hosted by Aunt Alexandra at the Finch house. The ladies of Maycomb, who, for the most part, stay silent during the book, come alive in these few pages; notably Mrs. Merriweather, who only stops her offensive dither to recharge, and Mrs. Farrow, "the second most devout lady" who speaks with "a soft sibilant sound," which in Lee's rendering means that she speaks like a snake. Very little actually happens here in this bewildering "world of women," where "fragrant ladies rocked slowly, fanned gently, and drank cool water" and the action lies in the subtext. This is the only time in the novel that the characters say exactly what they do not mean. Yet the tension is so evident that even Scout senses it; it is also a tension so dense that one cannot see, move, or breathe. In Scout's words, "Ladies in bunches always filled me with vague apprehension and a firm desire to be elsewhere." It turns out that her apprehension is well justified and not just the everyday restlessness of a little tomboy.

The ladies have gathered to proclaim their indignation at the squalid life lead by the Mrunas, in Africa. This is a classic ironic device: morally overblown people that cast their attentions to the troubles in foreign lands so that they can shut their eyes to the problems at home. Mrs. Merriweather states what is in many ways the motto of Maycomb: "Well I always say forgive and forget, forgive and forget. . . . If we just let them know we've forgiven 'em, we've forgotten it, then this whole thing will blow over." The citizens of Maycomb have always willed themselves to forget anything unpleasant, which is why they will never learn.

During the tea party, Mrs. Merriweather insults Atticus, but in a backhanded way. "Now far be it for me to say who, but there's some of 'em in this town thought they were doing the right thing a while back, but all they did was stir 'em up." At this point, Miss Maudie snaps. She herself is schooled in doublespeak, so she retorts in a way that is suitably difficult to understand. "His food doesn't stick going down, does it?" she remarks, referring to Atticus's untainted conscience. Her words are lost on Scout entirely, but the gaze of gratitude that Alexandra gives Maudie is not lost on her young niece. It is a blazing gesture of honesty in a cold, untruthful environment.

Atticus arrives home in the middle of the tea party with news of Tom, who was shot to death while attempting to escape from prison. Alexandra and Maudie, together with Calpurnia, find themselves united, and this time not by glances and double entendres. When Alexandra calls Atticus "brother," Scout realizes that she has arrived in the household, not for reasons of her own, but for the sake of the family, and most importantly, for that of her younger sibling. Miss Maudie, rather significantly, unties Calpurnia's apron for her as she prepares to go to the Robinsons. In the end, Miss Maudie and Aunt Alexandra clean their faces and resume their church tea party as if nothing has happened—all of the time, with their hearts plagued, but deriving strength from the other's presence.

Such an alliance—between Miss Maudie and Aunt Alexandra, who up until now could not have been more different—is somehow more poignant, and certainly more thoroughly realized, than Mr. Cunningham calling off the lynch mob with a wave of his hand. This, for more than anyone else, is Aunt Alexandra's moment. She has never consciously been a champion for right—what concerns her is propriety and background. But her devotion to Atticus, though unstated, is pure, and it is that devotion that opens her eyes. "It tears him up," she says, a woman who cannot fully express her emotions, yet loves her brother all the same, " . . . [This town] is perfectly willing to let him do what they're afraid to do themselves." She still might not understand the right that Atticus is trying to represent, but she does acknowledge her little brother as a hero. And with those words, Alexandra takes a stand and redeems herself.

The third section (chapters 26–31) of the novel is not openly indicated, but there is a clear break in the action between chapters 25 and 26. Just as Atticus has feared,

Maycomb returns swiftly to normal. "Maycomb," Lee writes, "was interested in the news of Tom's death for perhaps two days." The Maycomb inhabitants have resumed their habit of examining injustices abroad—Adolf Hitler has taken control of Germany. In chapter 26, a schoolteacher who had earlier commented about how the blacks were getting above themselves, lectured the children about the wrongs of Nazi Germany and prejudice. As Scout says, " . . . how can you hate Hitler so bad an' then turn around and be ugly about folks right at home. . . ."

Then the time frame shifts to an evening in October, when there is a Halloween pageant and Scout is to appear with the third grade dressed as a ham. Mortification sets in early, for Scout falls asleep backstage, misses her cue, and is scolded by her teacher. Scout mistakenly assumes that this is the worst thing that can happen to her that night. However, while walking home from the pageant, Jem and Scout are beset by Bob Ewell, who attacks them with the intention to kill. But they are mysteriously rescued. Scout escapes with a few scratches, and Jem is carried home unconscious with the same broken arm described at the novel's beginning, and Mr. Ewell is discovered dead with a knife in the ribs. Their hero turns out to be the children's alleged bogeyman, Boo Radley, and the story has come full circle. Bob Ewell pays for Tom Robinson's death with his own life. Most importantly, his end serves as a memorial to Tom in a town that has forgotten him. The one remaining victim of vicious gossip, Boo, has revealed himself as not only very much a human being but as the savior of children.

Most critics have described the concluding segment as the weakest, mixing disparate elements—political commentary, slapstick humor, and violence—in a sequence of events that proceeds at a frenetic pace. Indeed, Lee seems to be rushing to tie up loose ends, and certainly the ending of *Mockingbird* is more surreal than anything that has preceded it. But there are glimpses of the same magic that infected the early third of the book. Some critics have argued that the events of Halloween are unbelievable, but in many ways they ring truer than

Atticus's speech to the courtroom, or Scout confronting the lynch mob. Much of what transpired at the Halloween party was taken from actual events.

During Lee's childhood in Monroeville, young Truman Capote threw a Halloween party in which many of the entertainments mirrored those in *Mockingbird*—the children bob for apples, and they also put their hands into cardboard boxes to touch mystery substances. What was significant was that Capote had invited both a black man and also the reclusive Sonny Boular, who as previously stated, most likely provided Lee with the model of Boo. The Ku Klux Klan threatened to invade, and eventually laid their hands on Sonny, who was making a rare appearance completely unrecognizable in a robot costume of cardboard and wire. The Klan, thinking they had found the black man they set out to find, was on the verge of hanging Sonny and the sheriff was nowhere to be found. Interestingly enough, it was Harper Lee's attorney father—Amasa Coleman Lee, allegedly the model for Atticus Finch—who stopped the Klan and humiliated them. According to Marianne Moates's account of Capote's Monroeville years, *A Bridge to Childhood*, he said, "You've scared this boy half to death because you wanted to believe something that wasn't true. You ought to be ashamed of yourselves." (Moates, 62) Purportedly, behind Amasa Lee stood the prominent citizens of the town, just as the sheriff Heck Tate and Judge Taylor would eventually stand behind Atticus. Of course, the truth of such memories is colored by the fiction that they have inspired—we have no idea how much the events of Capote's party have hence been confused with the events in *Mockingbird*. Nevertheless, it demonstrates how sometimes the commotion of real life is often wilder than fiction. In real life, misery, sweetness, and violence often occur in the same breath. Halloween in *Mockingbird* is an odd night, but it feels less contrived than much of the book precisely because it is so strange.

Mockingbird also closes with a hint of uneasiness, which is unusual for a book that, up until this point, has been secure in its convictions. When Atticus believes that it is

Jem, now unconscious and unable to say what happened, who is responsible for Mr. Ewell's death, he seems willing to try his teenage son. True, this is also the man who would guard over his son all night and "would be there when Jem waked up in the morning." But Atticus mulls over whether Jem will be tried before the county court: "Best way to clear the air is to have it out in the open . . . I can't live one way in town and another way in my home." He is a man with a good heart and a just conscience; his balanced sense of right makes him incapable of the tenderness that possesses most fathers. When Sheriff Heck Tate insinuates that it is Boo, and not Jem, who is the guilty party, the dialogue reverses direction. For Tate ultimately convinces Atticus to state that Ewell fell on his knife, and Atticus turns his back on the central force in the book and in his life—the law. This is the man who once claimed that the beauty of the court lay in its ability to make all men equal, that it was the "one human institution that makes the pauper the equal of a Rockefeller, the stupid man the equal of an Einstein, and the ignorant man the equal of any college president." In the final pages of *Mockingbird*, this institution appears to be fallible. Its fall is foreshadowed when Jem shouts, "I don't wanta hear about that courthouse again, ever, ever, you hear me?"—a cry from a boy who has always looked up to the law. In the end, even Atticus has to own that, though the law is a great equalizer in theory, there are men who are superior to it and can make decisions without it. They do not include the Ewells, they do not even include honest farmers like Mr. Cunningham; it is an elite circle which seems to include Atticus and Heck Tate only.

The dialogue between the sheriff and Atticus is, as in several other passages in the book, obscure. One has a better sense reading it quickly; once it is subjected to scrutiny, it becomes confusing—there are too many gaps, too many insinuations, too many seemingly irrelevant statements. But the attack scene is also baffling in the same way; we do not know what is happening because we are only experiencing it from Scout's point of view—terrified for her life and half-blind in her ham costume. Similarly, Atticus and Tate's talk is reported from

Scout's perspective. In many ways, it reads much more like the memory of an eavesdropping little girl than her account of Tom Robinson's trial. She does not quite comprehend the whole, but she gets a sense of the important points.

Joyfully, Lee lets us become children again in part 3; we have returned to her fantastic and sometimes merciless fairy-tale world. But where in the beginning children acted out adventures in their imaginations, the happenings in part 3 are arguably satisfying because they are a children's adventure in the flesh. The denouement—Boo stepping into the light—is true to this storybook quality. It is not the most believable moment, but after the somber events of the trial and its aftermath, there is something refreshing about the ogre stepping out of the castle and revealing himself as a prince. These last ringing moments are gloriously true to Scout, who, after all, is still a little girl who believes, even after the past three years, that "nothin's real scary, except in books." So there are no grand adult moral statements to finish *To Kill a Mockingbird*, just the observation that "there wasn't much else to learn, except algebra." The melancholy that haunts these last few pages is poignant because it seems birthed from a genuine child's understanding.

> Neighbors bring food with death and flowers with sickness and little things in between. Boo was our neighbor. He gave us two soap dolls, a broken watch and chain, a pair of good luck pennies, and our lives. But neighbors give in return. We never put back into the tree what we took out of it; we had given him nothing, and it made me sad.

Small children do not feel tragedies on a large scale, they experience tragedy through the people and things with which they are intimate, and then rebound with incredible resilience. Scout's lesson, her "coming of age" moment is appropriate for a child her age.

In tone, and particularly concerning the central drama of Tom Robinson, the book is triumphant rather than tragic. This is despite Tom's death and not just because Ewell receives his comeuppance at the end. Atticus has fought on the side of right and, in his own way, has won. He never thought that he would win the trial in the first place, but there was always the possibility of an appeal and most importantly, it had opened the eyes of this sleepy town for an instant. Though Tom is convicted, the black community still honors him; they stand in unison as he passes. The jury is out for a few hours rather than the few minutes that Atticus is expecting. The fact that there are other people in Maycomb who are on the side of right is also a small victory—happily, as Miss Maudie points out to Jem, they include society's most important figures—the local judge and sheriff. There is also a Cunningham on the jury—one of the same men who had tried to lynch Tom just days before—who is "rarin'" for a complete acquittal. As Jem says, "One minute they're tryin' to kill him and the next they're tryin' to turn him loose." Then there is the Maycomb reporter Braxton Underwood, who, in Atticus's words, "despises Negroes . . . he won't have one near him." Nonetheless, just as Maycomb has almost forgotten Tom's death, Underwood writes a lengthy editorial in which he compares "Tom's death to the senseless slaughter of songbirds by hunters and children." Also, most of Maycomb might have forgotten Tom, but "Tom was not forgotten by his employer Mr. Link Deas." The person who benefits from this is Tom's widow. Deas hires her as a cook but also confronts and threatens Bob Ewell when he tries to harass her. Ultimately, it is Bob Ewell who loses. Even though he has received the guilty verdict that he demanded, he gains none of the respect that he was hoping the verdict would bring him, just as Price and Bates had hoped during the Scottsboro trials. " . . . [H]e'd thought he'd be a hero," says Atticus. Instead he is publicly humiliated, sent back to his squalor and, if anything, more despised than before. No one listening to the testimony could doubt that he is the guilty party. Even after Tom's death, Atticus can still be amused by the expression on Judge Taylor's face. "I proved him a liar but John made him look like a fool . . . John looked at him as if he were a three-legged chicken or a square egg." If Maycomb forgets Tom Robinson, they also forget Bob Ewell, and all his lunatic attempts to keep himself remembered are just laughed at by the genteel community that he hates.

The film version of *Mockingbird* (1962), which is by and large faithful to the spirit of the book, turns Tom's death into the central tragedy for which there is no redemption except Bob Ewell's death—a sort of poetic justice. Needless to say, Ewell's death is fate, whereas the true triumphs in the book are born of purposive human accomplishment. The intent of Atticus to fight for Tom, and that of Link Deas to protect Helen Robinson, are *Mockingbird's* victories, covered in the novel but skipped in the film. One reason there is such a discrepancy between the film and the book's treatment of Tom's death is the timing of events. In the movie, Tom's death immediately follows the verdict. Atticus and his children are walking home from the trial when they hear the news. There is no time to reflect, no time to understand the little ways in which Atticus wins. Though Tom's death is called "senseless" in the book, it does bring some sense to the town, and *Mockingbird* makes this clear in glancing ways. But the movie does not contain these intimations. We are left instead with the plain fact of an honest man murdered without good reason, leaving a wife and children behind.

"This may be a shadow of a beginning," Atticus says, and that is all he can hope for in Maycomb. What he considers a victory in the courtroom is telling of the time period in which the novel is set. Leaving a jury out for hours when before they would have been out for minutes—even if they deliver a guilty verdict in the end—is a rare occurrence for 1930s Alabama. The movie, on the other hand, is much more attuned to a turbulent 1960s spirit. Tom's conviction, and ultimately his death, are nothing short of horrible. It is in these glimpses of a beginning, these barely perceptible sunbeams that are overlooked by people and certainly not bright enough to be captured on celluloid, that are the triumphs of the literary embodiment of Atticus Finch. Fortunately, he is astute enough to recognize them himself.

Social Implications: Race, Class, and Gender

To Kill a Mockingbird illustrates the effects of prejudice on society. In Maycomb, the blacks ride in the backseats, live on the outskirts of town, have segregated sections in public spaces, and come into contact with white folks only in their jobs as cooks, trash collectors, and cotton pickers. As far as their church is concerned, "Negroes worshiped in it on Sundays, and white men gambled in it on weekdays." But prejudice is not limited to race. *Mockingbird* addresses all types of bigotry—those engendered by class, sex, and religion. Scout will never grow to be anything but a lady, though she wears overalls in childhood. Jem taunts Scout by calling her Angel May when she is reluctant to break into the Radley house, saying, "I declare to the Lord, you're gettin' more like a girl every day!" Similarly, Aunt Alexandra will not have young Walter Cunningham come to the Finches for supper because he is "trash." While blacks keep their separate quarters, so tenant farmers dwell in the woods, and the "white trash" beyond that—in the "dump" where they live in ugly, filthy hovels. While men may better themselves spiritually in *Mockingbird*, it is nearly impossible to improve socially.

Even the best of people are allowed their prejudices. Miss Maudie may respect Boo Radley but places the blame on "Old Mr. Radley" and his "footwashing Baptist" ways. This is an example of resentment characterized by Christian superiority. The view is that everyone should be a practicing Christian and attend church, for Christianity is as much a social practice as it is a sacred one—indeed, there are many sects in white Maycomb, and they are all friendly, with the women from all sects congregating for tea. One should not worship at home or carry beliefs to the extreme, both of which the Radleys are guilty of. Atticus, who, it seems, can look kindly upon a lynch mob, is satisfied with the way the townspeople tell Bob Ewell to " . . . get back to your dump." Indeed, Miss Maudie's behavior in her garden is a perfect metaphor for her and Atticus's attitude toward the community:

> She loved everything that grew in God's Earth, even the weeds. With one exception. If she found a blade of

nut grass in her yard, it was like the Second Battle of the Marne, she swooped down upon it with a tin tub and subjected it to blasts from beneath with a poisonous substance she said was so powerful it'd kill us all if we didn't stand out of the way.

Miss Maudie hates nut grass because one sprig can contaminate an entire yard, just as a weed like Bob Ewell can poison a town. Hence, the most generous of human beings—in this case Atticus and Miss Maudie—have their "one exception." For this, Lee does not condemn them. There is always one danger that no one can overcome. It is telling that both Miss Maudie's and Atticus's prejudices—against "footwashing Baptists" and "white trash" respectively—are appropriate to the convention that *To Kill a Mockingbird* endorses.

For in many ways, *To Kill a Mockingbird* is deeply conventional—albeit liberally conventional—for its time. Lee did not write her novel in Alabama, she wrote it in New York City at a time when it was not uncommon for liberal college educated elites—from the North and the South—to take an interest in African-American rights. Most of the outrage the book engendered was due to its focus on rape and not to its sympathetic portrayal of blacks. Ironically, there was outrage from the African-American community itself, for the novel's free use of the word *nigger*, though Lee portrays black characters in a sympathetic light.

Race relations had always been a problem for the South, but there was also an increased paranoia about poor whites as well. The South was decaying still, but its decay was blamed on white poverty infiltrating the genteel classes. Prevalent in *Mockingbird* is what is commonly called the "New South question." Fred Erisman, in his essay "The Romantic Regionalism of Harper Lee," eloquently argues that Lee believes that the New South is only possible if it incorporates "the New England romanticism of an Emerson." (Erisman, 46) But Lee believes also in the mores of the Old South—not its bigotry but its tradition, dignity, and romance. Maycomb stews in a "narcisstic regard for the warts and pimples in the past" (Erisman, 48) in part because it has lost its pre–Civil War pride. Erisman may believe that Lee advocates a breakdown of the class structure she details in *Mockingbird*, but in many ways *Mockingbird* upholds it. The reader should note that those who lobby for racial change are upper-middle class, notably Atticus Finch and Judge Taylor, who appoints Atticus to defend Tom. Tolerance, therefore, can only come via such men—products of a genteel background; it does not come from the farmers and certainly not from the "white trash." In fact, the elites are essential to resolving not only the race problem but the problem of the South itself.

To Kill a Mockingbird demonstrates that there are two kinds of gentility in the world—inherited and natural. Young Chuck Little, for instance, may be six years old and not know "where his next meal was coming from," but in Scout's words, he is "a born gentleman," and even a hulking brute like Burris Ewell respects him. Similarly, Calpurnia is a lady, and Tom Robinson's manners are "as good as Atticus's." Nevertheless, Chuck Little is still a tenant farmer's son who will never have Scout Finch over for supper, and Tom, even to Atticus, is still a "boy," even though he has a wife and three children. Nineteen-year-old Mayella is a "woman." To call a grown black man a "boy" was to judge him inferior to white men and women, which many people believed at this time.

The Finches descend from a noble background; not only are they born to it, they reflect this status in their behavior and conduct. The upper class is also populated with Mrs. Merriweathers and Miss Crawfords, who may have inherited an advantage but do not conduct themselves with propriety. Mrs. Dubose, on the other hand, is a different case altogether. She may not be the friendliest of human beings—indeed she is a cantakerous, bigoted annoyance—but when Atticus sends Jem over to read to her on her deathbed, he is not just doing it out of pity, Atticus actually holds Mrs. Dubose in high esteem. Mrs. Dubose, during her last few months, was a morphine addict; Jem's weekly sessions helped her break free of her addiction. "You know," Atticus tells Jem, "she was a great lady . . . According to her views, she died beholden to nothing and nobody. She was the bravest person I ever knew." Mrs. Dubose is the Old South, represented by the camellias that she grows—fragrant, tradition-bound, and waxy as death. She may represent the South's prejudice and its ugliness but also stand for its pride and willpower. Atticus may see the promise of the New South in his children, for they, in their innocence and openness, represent the kind of New England romanticism that critic Fred Erisman discusses; but he sees Mrs. Dubose as necessary to that New South as well.

Another character integral to the rise of the New South is Dolphus Raymond, the local eccentric who rarely comes into town and who carries a brown paper bag that smells of whiskey. Cloaked by a similar aura of mystery that surrounds Boo Radley, he lives in the black neighborhood with his black mistress and mixed children, and rumor has it that he is an "evil man." In the end, however, Raymond reveals himself as a drinker of cola rather than of whiskey and also as a source of wisdom. He pretends to be an alcoholic because "it's mighty helpful to folks . . . they could never, never understand that I live like I do because that's the way I want to live." He understands about "the simple hell people give other people—even without thinking."

Raymond takes a different approach from Atticus in society. Rather than taking a stand for what is right, he hides; it is what ultimately makes Atticus a nobler man because, unlike Raymond, Atticus is "the same man in his house as he is on public streets." Yet there is something endearing about Raymond, peacefully living with his biracial family, in many ways living the same way that Calpurnia has instructed Scout: "It's not necessary to tell all you know . . . when they don't want to learn there's nothing you can do but keep your mouth shut . . ." It goes without saying that this man is also its largest landowner, and his breeding is so evident that Scout can smell it. "I liked his smell," she confesses, "it was of leather, horses, cottonseed. He wore the only English riding boots I had ever seen." In certain ways he is Maycomb's most radical citizen and a perfect example of mixing new ways with the old.

Dolphus Raymond can live the way he wants because he is rich. Maycomb's poor, on the other hand, have no such choice. While the tenant farmers try to maintain their decency, there is another class—that of the "white trash"—that is simply irredeemable. This is already clear in the first grade classroom when Burris Ewell spits at the teacher and calls her "a snot-nosed slut." It is as if the "white trash" attitude is knit into these people at birth—a rather harsh assertion for what has been such a compassionate book. According to Atticus, "you never really know a man until you stand inside his shoes and walk around in them." Atticus can forgive a lynch mob; he can even tell his children not to hate Hitler. But Atticus does not step inside Bob Ewell's shoes, let alone try. A poor white man like Bob Ewell is Atticus's "one exception." He cannot be saved.

Social status in *Mockingbird* is a lifelong classification; you can work to improve your station, but you cannot transcend it. This is part of Mayella Ewell's downfall—she has lofty ambitions of rising above her station. Bob Ewell may want the town's attention, but Mayella wants more. She wants to be a dignified southern lady. In lieu of this wish, she grows geraniums "cared for as tenderly as Miss Maudie Atkinson had Miss Maudie Atkinson deigned to permit a geranium on her premises." Geraniums are not a lady's flower, but they make Mayella's pathetic effort to imitate her betters all the more poignant. Victoria Price and Ruby Bates in Scottsboro were cleaned up for court—these women of dubious virtue were bathed, dressed, and perfumed to look like respectible citizens, so that their purported rape would seem an attack on the ladylike chasteness that was such a factor in southern gender identity. Similarly, Mayella in court "looked as though she tried to keep herself clean" and seems "somewhat fragile-looking," but as she seats herself she becomes what she is—"a thick-bodied girl accustomed to strenuous labor."

Despite Atticus's assertion that the court system is our great social evener, at the end of *Mockingbird*, it is clear that the public courts may not hold the answer to everything. Hence, when Bob Ewell is stabbed, the "good" Heck Tate and Atticus Finch look away. People with the breeding to know can, in fact, serve justice; and looking after the town is the responsibility of upstanding citizens. Shouldering such responsibility is a complicated business, and is similarly laden with conduct codes and rules such as having "compn'y." Having someone over for "compn'y" is a subtle way of asserting superiority, because one can afford to extend graciousness; guests can behave however they like, but the hosts must have manners. The Finches can have Walter Cunningham to supper, but the Cunninghams will never have the Finches. Scout is slapped because she is rude to young Walter at the dinner table, when she is expected to behave with the propriety becoming a hostess. This also explains why Alexandra is upset when Cal takes the children to her church, and why she forbids Scout to be Cal's guest ever again, for Cal has tipped the social balance by playing the hostess. Calpurnia, in the church, forbids Jem to contribute to the collection plate with his own money. But the hierarchy between the children and Cal is gently restored when Jem proffers his and Scout's money the second time the collection plate comes around. Men like Atticus are like benevolent hosts, and Maycomb is their permanent company. It is of the utmost importantance for Atticus and his children to conduct themselves with grace.

After Tom's trial, Jem says to Scout, "There are four kinds of folks in the world. There's the ordinary kind like us and the neighbors, there's the kind like the Cunninghams out in the woods, the kind like the Ewells down at the dump, and the Negroes." Scout concludes, after a lengthy discussion, "Naw Jem, I think there's just one kind of folks. Folks." Jem responds, "That's what I thought, too, when I was your age." It is a simple scene, disarming because moral issues are being debated from a child's perspective. It is also a narrative crux. Scout's argument is from the innocent's perspective—what we want to be true but we know is not. Jem is wiser; he is beginning to realize that there are stratifications in this world, which cause hate, and the only hope for those who want to make a difference is to learn how to operate within the system.

Born as they are to the Maycomb upper class, Jem will grow up to be a gentleman and Scout to be a lady, and they both must take on the duties that their respective roles require. While we have a pretty good idea of what is expected of Jem from his father's legacy, Scout's future is less clear; but in many ways, it is just as demanding. The women of the community are crucial to the backbone of Maycomb. This is not to say that *Mockingbird* is a feminist text. Jem is encouraged to be a lawyer while Scout is not. (Lee, incidentally, attended law school in Alabama and her older sister became one of the most widely recognized attorneys in the South.) Atticus cheerfully remarks that if women were allowed on juries, "I doubt if we'd ever get a case tried—the ladies'd be interrupting to ask questions." But aristocratic southern women are a formidable presence in *To Kill a Mockingbird*, and if Scout has a quest in the novel, it is in recognizing the true ladies from the false, and in appreciating a true lady's value.

Ladylike conduct comes with an overwhelming number of rules that often contradict one another. Naturally, tomboy Scout, who is without girlfriend, sister, or mother, is revolted by what she regards as her "pink cotton penitentiary" fate. She is bewildered and frightened by her Aunt Alexandra's teaching. Being a lady, in Scout's mind, seems to entail not wearing pants, not associating with "trash,"

> playing with small stoves and tea sets and wearing the Add-A-Pearl necklace she gave me when I was born; furthermore that I should be a ray of sunshine in my father's lonely life.

When Scout, quite reasonably, points out that she can be a ray of sunshine in overalls as well as skirts, Aunt Alexandra cannot provide her with a satisfactory answer, so she scolds Scout instead. What Scout realizes by the end, however, is that being a lady is something that is at once simpler to understand and more challenging to undertake. It is about being subtle and modest while maintaining one's integrity. As Cal tells her, "It's not necessary to tell all you know. It's not lady like."

Not until the Missionary Ladies' tea party does Scout arrive at this realization. Mrs. Merriweather and the ladies of

Maycomb may outwardly depict the refinements of southern womanhood, with their glossy nails and murmuring voices. Scout had always viewed them as feminine paradigms; but some of the ladies of Maycomb can be vindictive and spiteful. Scout comes to learn that there is a difference between restraining oneself and being dishonest, between gentle criticism and virulent stabs in the back. A true lady does not insult her hostess's brother when he is not there to defend himself, as Mrs. Merriweather does. Kinship is forged between Aunt Alexandra and Miss Maudie when they recognize each other as the only other women of character on the porch:

> Aunt Alexandra got up from the table and swiftly passed the refreshments, neatly engaging Mrs. Merriweather and Mrs. Gates in brisk conversation. When she had them well on the road to Mrs. Perkins, Aunt Alexandra stepped back. She gave Miss Maudie a look of pure gratitude and I wondered at the world of women.

Later, Scout sees Aunt Alexandra pull herself together with Miss Maudie's curt assistance and smilingly returns to passing out teacakes. A true person of character never exposes herself, but inside, she remains true among the hypocrites. Mrs. Dubose is ultimately a great lady and Mrs. Merriweather is not, for Mrs. Dubose is honest. To carry on despite a broken heart, as Aunt Alexandra does that afternoon, can be as courageous as shooting a mad dog on a February day. For the first time, Scout is suitably impressed: " . . . if Aunty could be a lady at a time like this, so could I."

Rape is a central element to *Mockingbird*. Hints of rape are characteristic throughout the novel; the subject is not limited to Mayella Ewell's circumstances. The razing of Miss Maudie's azaleas by fire and of Miss Duboses's camellias by Jem are examples of rape symbolism. (Tellingly, Miss Maudie, who personifies the promise of the New South, springs back with optimism, while Miss Dubose, the old South, is thirsty for revenge.) The citizens of Maycomb are eager to blame

Mayella's rape on Tom Robinson because they want to blame the Old South's decay on the black population. That the perpetrator is obviously Bob Ewell is telling of Lee's own class paranoia: poor whites of dubious character, or "white trash," and not blacks, are responsible for the "rape" of the southern way of life.

Though there is a strong consensus that *To Kill a Mockingbird* is deeply oriented within the history of the Depression era, no analysis has attempted to separate the historical conditions of the moment of the text's production in the mid 1950s from the historical present of the novel, the mid 1930s. Such analysis is revealing, first because under scrutiny the novel's 1930s history is exposed as at times quite flawed in its presentation of facts. The WPA, for example, did not exist until 1935, but it is mentioned in the novel's fourth chapter, which is set in 1933. Eleanor Roosevelt did not violate segregation law by sitting with black audience members at the Southern Conference on Human Welfare in Birmingham until 1938, but this event is mentioned by Mrs. Merriweather during the fall of 1935. More important than these several occasional chronological lapses, however, is the novel's participation in racial and social ideology that characterized not the Depression era but the early civil rights era. Because the text's 1930s history is superficial, the novel is best understood as an amalgam or cross-historical montage, its "historical present" diluted by the influence of events and ideology concurrent with its period of production. The 1954 *Brown v. Board of Education* decision, for example, stimulated a national debate in which Lee's novel participates and upon which it offers forceful commentary. As fundamental a presence in *To Kill a Mockingbird* is the structural and ideological detail of the Emmett Till trial of 1955,[1] which upon close consideration seems unquestionably to have provided a workable model for aspects of Lee's fictional Tom Robinson trial. In other words, racial events and ideology of the 1950s—the period concurrent with the novel's production—leach into the depiction of Lee's 1930s history, orienting large sections the text not to the Depression era but to social conditions of the civil rights era. The mid 1950s/early civil rights era is therefore the context from which the novel is best understood as the intersection of cultural and literary ideology.

Lee herself hints at the contradictions contained within conflicting historical periodicity when she informs the reader early in the novel that its events are depicted from a somewhat distant perspective, "when enough years had gone by to enable us to look back on them" (3). Simply because neither the author nor even Scout, her first-person narrator and authorial surrogate, can experience the 1930s within the 1930s but must interpret from a later moment invested with its own discrete historical perspective, historical prolepsis—the representation or assumption of a future act or development as if presently existing or accomplished—is inevitable, and it is an indication that Lee's 1930s historical background, though developed in some detail, should not be allowed to obscure the real conditions which governed the text's production in the years from roughly 1955 to 1959.

Central issues of Harper Lee's fictional Tom Robinson case, along with cultural tensions ascendant in the aftermath of the May 17, 1954 *Brown v. Board of Education* decision, are located in the story of Emmett Till, a 14-year-old boy from Chicago who was brutally murdered by two white men in the Mississippi Delta on August 28, 1955 for allegedly whistling at a white woman in a store in Money, Mississippi. There is a long list of similarities both circumstantial and deeply ideological between the 1955 lynching of Emmett Till and Lee's account of the conviction and murder of Tom Robinson, similarities which point to the common origin of both texts in a particularly troubled period in the southern history of race.

During the mid to late 1950s, race relations in the Deep South were of course defined and dominated by the *Brown* decision, which negated the doctrine of "separate but equal" that had since *Plessy v. Ferguson* been the basis of the South's segregated way of life. Prior to the 1954 decision, what Benjamin Muse has called an "unwholesome stability" (1) had prevailed in the South, depriving nearly all blacks of the right to vote and adhering to strict and inviolable *de facto* and *de jure* segregation of the races in all areas of social life in which mixing of any kind could result in the suggestion of social equality.

The business of "keeping the negro in his place" (Muse 39) had for centuries been a major concern in the South, but *Brown v. Board of Education* greatly exacerbated the southern fears relating to racial mixing, amalgamation, and expectations of social equality for blacks, creating what Newby terms a "a new racism" (10) that directly responded to the Supreme Court's authority by "recasting old ideas to meet a new national mood" (10). In the immediate aftermath of decision, the Deep South exhibited the paranoia of a closed society that could not distinguish the defense of a "'few social areas' from the entire structure of white supremacy" (Whitfield 11). The preservation of white patriarchy "seemed to require the suppression of even the most insignificant challenges to authority" (11). The rising influence and activism of the NAACP resulted not only in the formation of the White Citizens Councils but production and dissemination of inflammatory anti-integration literature, organization of anti-integration rallies, intimidation of the small number of blacks who had registered to vote, condemnation of the "liberals and do-gooders" in both the South and in Washington, and the implicit call for violent resistance to the idea of school integration.

Foremost among all latent and overtly expressed fears that were directly intensified by the *Brown* decision was that surrounding interracial sex. Gunnar Myrdal's exhaustive 1947 study of southern culture had asked white southerners to choose among six categories in gauging what they believed blacks most desired by asserting their civil rights. First in ranking came "intermarriage and sex intercourse with whites" (Myrdal 58). It is indisputable that the *Brown* decision, ostensibly about school desegregation, was actually understood by many in the South as a dangerous amelioration of deadly serious taboos regarding sexual relations between black males and white females. . . .

In the context of the *Brown* decision, mixed schooling therefore meant much more than the implication of social equality. President Eisenhower may have inadvertently verbalized some of the deepest fears of southerners when he explained in 1954 that segregationists "were not bad people. All they are concerned about is to see that their sweet little girls are not required to sit in schools along side some big overgrown negroes" (qtd. in Whitfield 72). . . .

The September 1955 trial of Roy Bryant and J.W. Milam for the murder of Emmett Till in retribution for allegedly whistling at and talking in a suggestive way to Carolyn Bryant was front page news throughout the country. When Bryant and Milam were found not guilty by an all-white, all-male jury that deliberated only 67 minutes—"it would have been a quicker decision, said the foreman, if we hadn't stopped to drink a bottle of pop" (Halberstam 441)—Milam and Bryant "stood acquitted in Mississippi and convicted by most of the nation" (441).

Graciously responding to my queries, Harper Lee has indicated that she was not in Mississippi in 1955 and was not present at the Emmett Till trial. But in order to be cognizant of the Till case and its meaning, she did not have to be. The Emmett Till trial, now forgotten by many, surprisingly absent from some recent histories, often ignored as one of the galvanizing events of the early civil rights movement, was in 1955 "probably the most widely publicized trial of the century" (Whitaker 148). Halberstam has termed it "an international incident" (432), " . . . the first great media event of the civil rights movement" (437). As the daughter of a well-known Southern attorney and a one-time law student from a family with a considerable legal background,[4] Harper Lee may be presumed to have taken an interest in the Till case, which was immediately identified as a monumental legal benchmark.[5] In 1975, for example, the founder of the Citizens Councils attempted to identify the moment when the civil rights movement began: "It all started probably with a case of a young Negro boy named Emmett Till getting killed for offending some white woman . . . that made every newspaper on the face of the earth . . ." (Whitaker 148). Largely due to what most historians refer to as a decline of "faith in legalism" at the unconscionable verdict of the Till trial, blacks in the South were moved to attempt more concrete forms of protest. Within four months after Till's death, Alabama blacks were staging the Montgomery bus boycott—the first major battle in the civil rights era war against racial injustice.

Commonalities in the Emmett Till trial and the trial of Tom Robinson in *To Kill a Mockingbird* have been suggested but nowhere investigated. . . .

The two cases are linked by numerous similarities of circumstance. Both cases combine the dual icons of the "black rapist" and concomitant fear of black male sexuality with mythologized "vulnerable and sacred" Southern womanhood. Both cases involve alleged transgressions of the strict inviolable mores barring social and sexual contact between black males and white females of any social class, for which, in both cases, the penalty is death for the black offender. Both cases are heard by all-white, all-male juries consisting primarily of Southern farmers. Both cases result in verdicts that preserve tenaciously held racial doctrine of the white power structure at the expense of justice and in the face of overwhelming contradictory evidence. In both cases a community of potentially fair-minded middle-class whites is required, against its initial leanings and for reasons perceived as the lesser of two evils, to support the obviously false testimony of a pair of otherwise-despised poor whites. In both cases, a courageous attorney and a fair-minded judge tacitly cooperate in a futile attempt to ensure justice. In both cases, the black victim is a diminished physical specimen of a fully grown man. In both cases, the press or media emerge as a force for racial justice. In both cases, the concept of child murder figures prominently in the calculus of revenge for the racial and social shame of a class of poor Southern whites.

The list of similarities could go on, eventually extending even into relatively minor surface details, such as the fact that Emmett Till was killed on August 28, 1955 and that his body was found on August 31, dates which turn out to be practically identical to the date of Tom Robinson's death, which took place when "August was on the brink of September" (228). . . .

By the end of Lee's novel then, the limitations of a particular and highly historically relevant ideological apparatus have been exposed, and the law is, even for Atticus, reduced to a ritual in which absolute faith is no longer possible. Through this process we perceive the potential instability of the structure of legal order in the South on the verge of the violent convulsions that attended the civil rights era. If the text here compels a consideration of the validity of subversive intervention, as it seems to have for at least some of Lee's contemporaries in the wake of the Emmett Till case, it is because, as Greenblatt explains, "power . . . is not perfectly monolithic and hence may encounter and record in one of its functions materials that can threaten another of its functions" ("Invisible Bullets" 50). "The simple operation of any systematic order . . . will inevitably run the risk of exposing its own limitations" (52). Because power "defines itself in relation to threats or simply to that which is not identical to it" (50), the full awareness of its effect requires what Greenblatt terms a collective "vigilance," the kind of vigilance, I would suggest, that is practiced by Sheriff Tate and Atticus, who sanction the personal subversion of an institutional power to which both men had earlier expressed and enacted allegiance. This transference contains a radical questioning that insists passionately on the efficacy of action in obedience to the private commands of conscience instead of reliance on more orthodox forms of redress.[11] In the "secret courts of men's hearts" (Lee 241), tainted as they are with virulent racial prejudice, neither Tom Robinson nor Emmett Till had any chance, but Lee's novel ends with the verdict of a secret court that, though it cannot restore the status quo ante by returning Tom Robinson to his family, does destroy the complicity between racism and a legal system that had been required to serve it—negating the very arrangement that had thwarted justice in the Robinson and Till cases.

Lee's novel therefore ends where the civil rights movement begins, with a resolve born of disillusionment to improvise ways and means of justice both within and outside a system that could convict Tom Robinson and acquit Emmett Till's murderers. In the presentation, discussion, containment and suppression of a court case pitting the state against Arthur Radley—a case that could have been but will not be—there is a conscious attempt to compensate for the disastrous effects of its antecedents in Tom Robinson and Emmett Till—court cases that could not have been but were. The text may be read as Lee's method of working out complex issues of conscience and subjectivity suggested by the Till case and the civil rights movement in general. Harper Lee's version of history, like the version of events agreed upon as the real story of Bob Ewell's death, is therefore not literally but symbolically "true," retold in a way that liberates the essential symbolic precepts from the less significant details of place, time, and circumstance while remaining passionately faithful to allegorical truth.

Notes

1. In August of 1955, fourteen-year-old Chicago native Emmett Till arrived in the Mississippi Delta to visit relatives in Tallahatchie County. On the evening of August 24, 1955, Till and his cousin Curtis Jones drove to a small grocery store run by Roy and Carolyn Bryant in the hamlet of Money. The initial incident is still the subject of debate. According to some accounts, he whistled at Carolyn Bryant. According to the testimony of Mrs. Bryant, Till grabbed her wrist and made a lewd suggestion before leaving the store. The murder trial took place in September of 1955. Though Moses Wright named in court the two white men who had taken Till from his shack, the all-white, all-male jury acquitted Milam and Bryant after deliberating 67 minutes. (For detailed accounts of the trial, see Whitfield, Halberstam, Whitaker.)

4. Claudia Durst Johnson has investigated connections between Lee's Robinson trial and the 1932–36 Scottsboro trials, which took place in Northern Alabama and involved allegations of gang rape of two white women by nine black men. "The central parallels between the novel and Scottsboro trials," Johnson argues, "are three: the threat of lynching; the issue of a Southern jury's composition; and the intricate symbolic complications arising from the interweave of race and class when a lower-class white woman wrongfully accuses a black man or men" (5). Though the similarities Johnson notes are intriguing, they are also, I would argue, superficial in comparison to those herein noted and less compelling in terms of historical relevance. Born in 1926, Harper Lee was five years old at the time of the Scottsboro incident. As I have here suggested, the novel's most definitive historical milieu is the 1950s, and the Emmett Till case a more powerful register of the racial ideology of that period.

5. Lee enrolled at the University of Alabama School of Law in 1947. She dedicated the novel to her father, Amasa Coleman Lee, a Monroeville attorney who served in the Alabama State Legislature from 1927 to 1939, and to her sister, Alice Lee, also a practicing

attorney. The novel's motto, "Lawyers, I suppose, were children once" (Charles Lamb), and the astute courtroom observations of its narrator also indicate a high level of legal knowledge and concern. Claudia Durst Johnson has noted that "the largest volume of criticism on the novel has been done by legal rather than literary scholars" (25).

11. Claudia Carter details the development of Atticus's legal outlook into "a compassionate activism . . . a model we can emulate" (13).

LAURIE CHAMPION ON THE MORAL MEANINGS OF "LEFT" AND "RIGHT" IN THE NOVEL

Throughout Harper Lee's *To Kill a Mockingbird*, besides the ordinary connotations of "right" and "left" as opposing spatial directions, the terms also work on a subtler level: "right" suggesting virtue and "left" suggesting iniquity.

Connotations of "right" and "left" play a crucial role during the climactic trial scenes. Building evidence against Bob Ewell, Atticus asks Sheriff Tate which one of Mayella's eyes was bruised the night she was attacked, and Tate replies, "Her left." Atticus asks, "Was it her left facing you or her left looking the same way you were?" (179). Tate says, "Oh yes, that'd make it her right. It was her right eye, Mr. Finch. I remember now, she was bunged up on that side of her face" (179). Bob says that he agrees with Tate's testimony that Mayella's "right eye was blackened" (187). A reading of the transcript of Tate's testimony reminds the jury that Tate testified that Mayella's right eye was black: "[W]hich eye her left oh yes that'd make it her right it was her right eye. [. . .] [I]t was her right eye I said—" (187). Directional words "right" and "left" are repeated, emphasizing the dichotomy. Literally, Mayella could not see clearly from her right eye when it was bruised; symbolically, Mayella cannot act morally.

Whereas Mayella's right eye is bruised, Atticus is nearly blind in his left eye, both literally and figuratively: "Whenever he wanted to see something well, he turned his head and looked from his right eye" (98). Later, when Atticus scolds Scout, he pins her "to the wall with his good eye" (146). When Atticus questions Mayella on the witness stand, he "turned his good right eye to the witness" (199). Atticus uses his "right" eye, his "good" eye for wisdom. Both "good" and "right" express moral undertones, as in "the good," suggesting wisdom and insight are products of "good" eyes.

Portrayals of Mayella's bruised right eye also contrast portrayals of Tom's left arm, which was "fully twelve inches shorter than his right, and hung dead at his side" (197). Tom's left arm "hung dead," just as immorality is dead in him. While the court observes Tom's mangled left arm, Atticus asks Mayella, "He blackened your left eye with his right fist?" (198–99). Atticus's point is made, and with repeated use of various connotations of words such as "left," "right," and "side," implications of morality abound.

Atticus proves Bob is left-handed, providing circumstantial evidence that Bob attacked Mayella. Atticus says, "Mayella Ewell was beaten savagely by someone who led almost exclusively with his left" (216). Bob signs a warrant "with his left hand," whereas Tom takes "the oath with the only good hand he possesses—his right hand" (216). Bob is "led" by the immoral left, but Tom tells the truth, swearing with his "good" right hand. Tom's "good arm" parallels Atticus's "good eye," and in both cases "good" signifies proper function and virtue.

Before Tom's mangled left arm is exposed, Scout questions Tom's innocence. She says that if Mayella's "right eye was blacked and she was beaten mostly on the right side of the face, it would tend to show that a left-handed person did it. [. . .] But Tom Robinson could easily be left-handed, too. Like Mr. Heck Tate, I imagined a person facing me, went through a swift mental pantomime, and concluded that he might have held her with his right hand and pounded her with his left" (189). Again, the words "right" and "left" are repeated. Scout also uses the word "facing," a directional word that represents the jury Tom faces and the truth the jury refuses to face.

Lee introduces a right–left dichotomy in the opening scene of *To Kill a Mockingbird*, a scene narrated many years after the events of the narrative proper. Scout says that Jem's "left arm was somewhat shorter than his right; when he stood or walked, the back of his hand was at right angles to his body [...]" (9). Jem, like Tom, has an injured left arm and a healthy right arm. His hand turns at right angles, signifying his morally correct perspective. In the opening paragraph, Scout provides a framework for her story, disclosing that she will explain how Jem's accident occurred. As the plot unravels, readers are told how Jem hurt his arm. More important, readers come to understand Jem's moral development.

Immediately after Atticus shoots a rabid dog, Sheriff Tate runs to Atticus and taps "his finger on his forehead above his left eye" (105). He says, "You were a little to the right, Mr. Finch." Atticus answers, "Always was [...]" (105). Of course, Tate refers to the direction "right" as opposed to "center" or "left," but symbolically, Atticus looks to the "right," protects the neighborhood. The dog "walked erratically, as if his right legs were shorter than his left legs" (101). The dog's lame right legs symbolize malevolence, his danger to society.

As in instances where "right" opposes "left," the term "right" designates that a specific spatial locale also has ethical undertones. Atticus tells Calpurnia that Tom stood "[r]ight in front of" the guards who shoot him (248). Tom stands both directly in front of the guards and on his own symbolic ethical ground. Inquiring if during the trial the children sat in the balcony of the courthouse, Miss Stephanie asks, "Wasn't it right close up there with all those—?" (227). Symbolically, "right" refers to the truth, the section of the courthouse where people sit who support Tom, Atticus, and racial equity.

The term "left" also denotes what remains, what is "left" of something. Scout says that the dog "had made up what was left of his mind," turned around and began to walk toward the Finch's house (105). A few paragraphs later, Lee contrasts Atticus's mind with the dog's mind. After learning Atticus had once been called "Ol' One-Shot [...] the deadest shot in Maycomb County" (106), Jem asks Miss Maudie why he never brags about his marksmanship talents. She answers, "People in their right minds never take pride in their talents" (107). Here, the "right" mind literally refers to people who think straight, level-headed people—in this case, implying that Atticus is humble. Whereas the dog uses what is "left" of his mind to harm people, Atticus, in his "right" mind, exemplifies humility.

Atticus, Tom, and Jem represent moral virtue: Atticus uses his "right" mind and his "good, right" eye to defend Tom; Tom takes the oath with his "good, right" hand; and Jem, with his vigorous "right" arm, defends Tom. Contrarily, the rabid dog, Mayella, and Bob represent moral inequity. The dog's "left" legs are healthy; Mayella's "left" eye is healthy; and Bob is "left" handed. The rabid dog presents a physical threat to Maycomb County, but Mayella and Bob present a social threat—the perpetuation of racism. Atticus's virtue only enables him to eliminate the physical threat. That the jury convicts Tom in the end signals that Atticus loses his battle against racism.

ISAAC SANEY ON RACISM IN *TO KILL A MOCKINGBIRD*

For many years the Black Educators' Association and parents, amongst others, have lobbied the Nova Scotia Department of Education and school boards to remove various books from the school curriculum and school use. Similar initiatives have taken place in New Brunswick and other provinces across Canada. Pressure from the community forced the Department of Education to face up to its social responsibility to provide enlightened education and teaching materials and address the issue of restricting racist materials in the province's classrooms, in the same way that pressure had forced the government to abandon its legislated policy of segregated schooling for the African Nova Scotian population, a policy only formally ended in the 1950s. In 1996, after intensive community pressure, three works—*To Kill a Mockingbird* by Harper Lee; *In the Heat of the Night* by John Dudley Ball; and *Underground to Canada* by Barbara Smucker—were taken off the authorised list of texts recommended by the Department of Education. They can no longer be purchased from the provincial government.

Six years later, in March 2002, the African-Nova Scotian ad hoc advisory committee (a committee of parents and educators) of the Tri-County district, which runs schools in southwestern Nova Scotia, recommended that the three works should be removed from school use altogether. Many educators consider these demands as minimal and as barely beginning to address the serious inequalities which continue to pervade the education system. Members of the Black Educators' Association (BEA) again seconded this specific recommendation. In the words of BEA director Gerry Clarke, a former school principal: 'It's demeaning and offensive to those students who have to put up with this.' Indeed, a 2000 report on *To Kill a Mockingbird* laid out the community's concerns:

> In this novel, African-Canadian students are presented with language that portrays all the stereotypical generalizations that demean them as a people. While the White student and White teacher may misconstrue it as language of an earlier era or the way it was, this language is still widely used today and the book serves as a tool to reinforce its usage even further ... The terminology in this novel subjects students to humiliating experiences that rob them of their self-respect and the respect of their peers. The word 'Nigger' is used 48 times [in] the novel ... There are many available books which reflect the past history of African-Canadians or Americans without subjecting African-Canadian learners to this type of degradation ... We believe that the English Language Arts curriculum in Nova Scotia must enable all students to feel comfortable with ideas, feelings and experiences presented without fear of humiliation ... *To Kill a Mockingbird* is clearly a book that no longer meets these goals and therefore must no longer be used for classroom instruction.[1] ...

Editorialists were especially incensed that *To Kill a Mockingbird* had come under criticism. The book was lauded as a classic, a paragon of anti-racist literature and, therefore, untouchable and sacrosanct.[8] The Black community was chided for being overly sensitive to the use of racial slurs and for its failure to appreciate the context and message of the novel. What was ignored was that the use of racist epithets or negative and debased imagery is not the only basis upon which to determine the racist or anti-racist character of a book. Jane Kansas, a columnist for the *Halifax Daily News*, typified the prevailing mindset. She, along with other partisans of the book, invoked the lecture Miss Maudie Atkinson delivers to Atticus Finch's daughter, Scout, on why it is 'a sin to kill a mockingbird'. This 'homily' was extolled as the most eloquent literary anti-racist statement.[9] Indeed, the lines define the book:

'Mockingbirds don't do one thing but make music for us to enjoy. They don't eat up people's gardens, don't nest in corncribs, they don't do one thing but sing their hearts out for us. That's why it's a sin to kill a mockingbird.'[10]

However, Kansas and others failed to explore the obvious meaning behind these words. Is not the mockingbird a metaphor for the entire African American population? Do these lines, as the partisans of the book assert, embody the loftiest ideals and sentiments? Harper Lee's motives notwithstanding, they are not a paean to the intrinsic equality and humanity of all peoples, nor do they acknowledge that Blacks are endowed with the same worth and rights as whites. What these lines *say* is that Black people are useful and harmless creatures—akin to decorous pets—that should not be treated brutally. This is reminiscent of the thinking that pervaded certain sectors of the abolition movement against slavery which did not extol the equality of Africans, but paralleled the propaganda of the Society for the Prevention of Cruelty to Animals, arguing that just as one should not treat one's horse, ox or dog cruelly, one should not treat one's Black cruelly.[11] By foisting this mockingbird image on African Americans, the novel does not challenge the insidious conception of superior versus inferior 'races', the notion of those meant to rule versus those meant to be ruled. What it attacks are the worst—particularly violent—excesses of the racist social order, leaving the racist social order itself intact. In short, as Malcolm X would probably have said, it presents the outlook of the 'enlightened' versus the 'unenlightened' slave owner, who wishes to preserve the value of his human property, the beasts of burden, to labour for his benefit, enjoyment and profit.

Central to the view that *To Kill a Mockingbird* is a solid and inherently anti-racist work is the role of Atticus Finch, the white lawyer who defends Tom Robinson, the Black man wrongly accused of raping a white woman. Indeed, Atticus goes so far as to save Tom from a lynching.[12] However, this act has no historical foundation. The acclaimed exhibition *Without Sanctuary: Lynching Photography in America*, sponsored by the Roth-Horowitz Gallery and the New York Historical Society, documented more than 600 incidents of lynching. This landmark exposition and study established that 'lynchers tended to be ordinary people and respectable people, few of whom had any difficulties justifying their atrocities in the name of maintaining the social and racial order and the purity of the Anglo-Saxon race'.[13] In two years of investigation, the exhibit researchers found no evidence of intervention by a white person to stop even a single lynching.

Perhaps the most egregious characteristic of the novel is the denial of the historical agency of Black people. They are robbed of their role as subjects of history, reduced to mere objects who are passive hapless victims; mere spectators and bystanders in the struggle against their own oppression and exploitation. There's the rub! The novel and its supporters deny that Black people have been the central actors in their movement for liberation and justice, from widespread African resistance to, and revolts against, slavery and colonialism to the twentieth century's mass movements challenging segregation, discrimination and imperialism. Yet, *To Kill a Mockingbird* confounds the relationship between whites of conscience and the struggles of the Black community. The novel is set in the 1930s and portrays Blacks as somnolent, awaiting someone from outside to take up and fight for the cause of justice. It is as if the Scottsboro case—in which nine young Black men travelling on a freight train in search of work were wrongfully convicted of raping two white women who were riding the same freight train—never happened. The trial was a 'legal lynching carried through with the cooperation of the courts and the law enforcement agencies'.[14] All but one were sentenced to death; the jury was hung on whether the ninth one should be sentenced to life imprisonment or death. The germane point is that a maelstrom of activity swept through African American communities, both North and South. They organised, agitated, petitioned and marched in support of and to free the nine young men. *To Kill a Mockingbird* gives no inkling of this mass protest and instead creates the indelible impression that the entire Black community existed in a complete state of paralysis. It was African North Americans who took up the task of confronting and organising against racism, who through weal and woe, trial and tribulation, carried on—and still carry on—the battle for equal rights and dignity. Those whites who did, and do, make significant contributions gave, and give, their solidarity in response.

Notes

1. 'A proposal regarding the usage of the novel: *To Kill a Mockingbird*' (Halifax, African-Canadian Services Division, Nova Scotia Department of Education and the Race Relations Coordinators in Nova Scotia, English program division of the Education Department, February 4, 2000).

8. 'Novel Dilemma'. *Chronicle Herald* (12 May 2002).

9. Jane Kansas, op. cit.

10. Harper Lee. *To Kill a Mockingbird* (London, Pan, 1981), p. 96.

11. See comment by Richard Hart in the documentary 'The Black Image: Representations of Africans in Europe throughout History' (London, Association for Curriculum Development, 1990).

12. Lee, op. cit., p. 154–8.

13. See James Allen and Leon F. Litwack, *Without Sanctuary: Lynching Photography in America* (Santa Fe, NM, Twin Palms. 2000).

14. Harry Haywood. *Black Bolshevik: Autobiography of an Afro-American Communist* (Chicago, Liberator Press, 1978).

Harper Lee's Pulitzer Prize–winning novel, *To Kill a Mockingbird*, charts the development of a young Southern girl from a childhood of innocence and freedom to an awareness of cruelty, evil, and the limitations and constraints of her position in her culture. The first-person narrative of Jean Louise "Scout" Finch reveals her unusually perceptive account of three significant years of her childhood. The setting of the novel, a small town in Alabama during the mid-1930s, and the central conflict, the trial of a Black man falsely accused of raping a white woman, create an intersection of the issues of race, class, and gender as Lee explores the dynamics of racial prejudice, Depression-era poverty, and genteel Southern womanhood.

The novel begins in the summer before Scout enters the first grade. Scout is a tough little tomboy who spends her days playing with her older brother Jem and her evenings reading with her father, Atticus Finch. Fiercely independent, Scout resists any kind of limitations placed upon her. The author establishes Scout's carefree existence in order to dramatize all that threatens to destabilize her protected view of herself and her community. Atticus Finch will defend Tom Robinson in his trial for the alleged rape of Mayella Ewell, and the events precipitated by the trial will destroy Scout's illusions, forcing her to reconsider everything she holds to be true—about human nature, about individual power, and about justice.

Scout's primary identification with the masculine world of her brother Jem and her father stems in part from her mother's death when Scout was only two. She has no memory of her mother, so she looks to Jem and Atticus as her guides to appropriate behavior. According to Scout, power and authority are masculine attributes; to be a girl is to be marginalized and excluded. An important part of Scout's development is her growing comprehension that she will be forced to enter the world of women, a world that holds no attractions for her. In her description of a typical summer day in Maycomb, Scout includes a portrait of a Southern lady: "Ladies bathed before noon, after their three-o'clock naps, and by nightfall were like soft teacakes with frostings of sweat and sweet talcum" (5–6). Her assessment of what it means to be a woman underscores her dismissal of an apparently useless, decorative existence.

Various female characters influence Scout's social development and exemplify the range of gender roles available to her. Additionally, they represent cultural distinctions determined by race and class. Scout's responses to these women reflect her growing knowledge of where power resides in her community. Calpurnia, the Finch family's African-American cook and housekeeper, provides a strong and loving female presence and acts as a role model for her, but Scout's relationship with Calpurnia is marked at first by conflict and rebellion. Over the course of the novel, however, she and Calpurnia grow closer. Although Calpurnia has some of the qualities of the stereotypical "Mammy" figure, Lee's characterization extends beyond that limited portrayal. Calpurnia has a life and a mind of her own, and she is the necessary transitional figure who moves comfortably through both sides of this racially divided Southern town. Taking Scout and Jem to her church with her one Sunday, Calpurnia exposes them to another side of racism in Maycomb—the hatred of some members of the Black community. While Calpurnia protects Scout from insults and violence, she also trains her to see the reality of the world around her. Calpurnia teaches the Finch children about their shared common humanity with their African-American neighbors, and she acts as both a moral guide and an example of female authority for Scout. When Jem and Dill eventually exclude her from their play, Scout discovers female companionship with Miss Maudie Atkinson, their iconoclastic neighbor, a widow who defies convention by tending her garden "in an old straw hat and men's coveralls" (47). Miss Maudie successfully balances an independent spirit with traditional gender roles and therefore becomes a strong potential role model for Scout.

As she observes the trial of Tom Robinson, Scout begins to discern differences in class in her hierarchical Southern community. Mayella Ewell, who has unjustly accused Tom

Robinson of rape, takes the stand and reveals her vicious racism, her ignorance, and the barren poverty of her existence.

Scout gradually begins to understand her own power and the power of women. During her father's confrontation with a group of vigilantes who come to lynch Tom Robinson, Scout single-handedly defuses the violence and shames the men by identifying them by name and asking about their families. Not all female power, however, is good. During the trial, it is clear to everyone that Mayella Ewell is lying, that she has accused Tom Robinson of rape to mask her own social crime of desire for a Black man. Yet the all-white jury finds him guilty despite evidence to the contrary. In this place and time, the word of a white woman counts more than that of a Black man. After the trial, Scout helps serve the women of the town at one of her Aunt Alexandra's "missionary circle" gatherings (261). There she witnesses the veiled but brutal and hypocritical pronouncements of racist white women intent on their so-called Christian duty.

Students respond with engagement to the conflicts presented in *To Kill a Mockingbird*. They may be offended by the use of racial epithets and the thinly veiled paternalism of the novel's white characters. In this racist Southern community, Atticus Finch is the moral center of the novel, and his attitudes and beliefs—about equality in the eyes of the law; about integrity, honesty, and fairness; and about the responsibility of those privileged by social status or race—become Scout's moral and ethical touchstone. The film version of the novel provides students with a memorable interpretation of the text and a visual frame of reference for the setting, but the movie's primary attention to the character of Atticus Finch detracts from the novel's narrative exploration of Scout's character development. Students may find it useful to compare the two characters as protagonists of the film and the novel.

Scout's narrative point of view is honest and often unintentionally humorous as she grapples for a complete understanding of her world. *To Kill a Mockingbird* can be read as a feminist *bildungsroman*, for Scout emerges from her childhood experiences with a clear sense of her place in her community and an awareness of her potential power as the woman she will one day be. Admittedly, her power is limited and her authority is circumscribed by the historical/cultural context of the novel; Lee's portrayal of Scout ends not in defeat but in a triumphant expansion of her knowledge, understanding, and sympathy.

Richard Armstrong on *Mockingbird* Lessons: Novel and Film

To Kill a Mockingbird owes its moral centre to Scout and to Mary Badham who played her. Badham was nine when she was nominated for an Oscar. Pulling off the complex assignment of playing a little girl with all the spirit and energy of a tomboy yet all the imagination and sensitivity of the woman Scout will become, Badham brings a favourite Hollywood screenwriter's model to life. Her performance is natural, assured and never cloying.

Sweet and caring, Scout is also crafty and rambunctious! At the heart of many scenes is her refusal to act like little girls are supposed to. . . .

Count up how many times you see Scout dashing along the streets of the town whilst adult extras sedately go about their business. At one point, she climbs inside an old truck tyre and Jem pushes it along the road, Scout rotating inside it. (The children constantly interact with their environment. How often do you see them swinging on gates or straddling railings? Do you remember taking your environment for granted as a child?)

When the lynch mob mass on the jail steps and threaten Atticus as he guards Tom before the trial, Scout races to be with him. As she charges through the mob we see the massed legs of the men as the camera barrels among them. As much of the film follows the children's adventures, we often see things at waist height. Their opinions and prejudices unavailable to the children, the men of the town seem mysterious and dangerous. Until the courtroom scene, Tom Robinson's story unfolds in scenes between adults, only becoming central to the film as she and Jem become curious about what's going on at the courthouse and Scout feels the prejudice of other children. We see Mr Cunningham (Crahan Denton) through her eyes as she speaks to him on the steps of the jail. It is a powerful scene, like others in the film dependent upon alignment of the audience's perspective with that of a child. Through a child's eyes, adults often seem inscrutable. Whilst Badham/Scout addresses Mr Cunningham straight to camera, Denton/Cunningham looks away, his hat obscuring his face. The tension in the scene arises from our being unsure what he is thinking or what he will do next. At last he looks straight at Scout and responds to her concern for him and his family: "Thank-you, young lady." By addressing Scout as "young lady," he acknowledges both her true gender and her more genteel social status. Mr Cunningham's words reinforce distinctions that the film is anxious to uphold.

Gender and Class

As the mature Jean Louise remembers her father saying: "You never really knew a man until you stood in his shoes and walked around in them." When we first meet Mr Cunningham, Scout learns that the Cunninghams are poor and poverty makes a proud man ashamed. When we next see Cunningham, he heads a lynch mob of farmers who, like him, were hit hardest by the Depression. Harper Lee's book was set during a period in American history when millions of men were out of work. Notice how in scenes with Cunningham Atticus stands on steps, raising him slightly above the other man. The actor placement suggests a difference in social standing between characters. Notice that the Finches always have plenty to eat. At one point, Scout brings Cunningham's son back for dinner. Look how much of everything there is as cinematographer Russell Harlan dwells on Atticus ladling sweet potato and spinach, the children tuck into plates of meat, and Cunningham Jr. drowns his meat in gravy!

Social standing is central to the problems the film works through. It is significant that traditional gender characteristics are deeply involved with one another in Scout, since the film is most poignantly about defining masculinity. *To Kill a Mockingbird* appeared at a time when millions of Americans were experiencing the most affluent and comfortable lives that any Americans had ever experienced. The economy was booming and unemployment was low. There was a young, dynamic and charismatic President Kennedy in the White House and much talk in academic circles of the "Affluent Society." America had come a long way in thirty years. For millions of Americans in the rich white suburbs of the 1960s this was how things should be and their values were the right values. The 1960s had seen the emergence of a college-educated white-collar class of lawyers, teachers and corporation executives whose trim grey suits and Kennedy crew cuts earned them the epithet "Corporation Man." Atticus does not belong to this generation, so does not conform to this image. But the film shows him as an educated man who can also act tough when necessary, answering whatever misgivings around the virility of the Corporation Man may have persisted in this traditionally masculine society.

Enjoying the highest standard of education provision in its history, in America in the 1960s language and literature were prized among the dominant middle class which comprised most of this film's audience. *To Kill a Mockingbird* compares Scout's environment, full of books and knowledge, with that of the Ewells and the Cunninghams in which more pressing needs have taken precedence. According to Jem, Scout had been reading "since she was born." Whilst the film illustrates Atticus and Scout's relatively affluent family life, we must infer from the court proceedings that Ewell sexually abuses Mayella and beats her when he is drunk. If Mayella is a gibbering idiot, Scout is a well-adjusted little girl, vindicating the liberal democratic ideal of a sensible diet, lots of affection, and a rounded education. One suspects that nobody ever called Mayella "young lady."

Most of *To Kill a Mockingbird* is shot in brightly lit stable compositions that suggest an objective 'normal' environment. But in certain scenes, the film mobilizes conventions that suggest more menacing characteristics. When Jem makes his way onto the porch of the old Radley place, an apparently dilapidated shack often accompanied by 'spooky' music, Boo's shadow passes over him in spine-chilling fashion. When Bob Ewell appears out of the gloom at the Robinsons, demented and clawing at the car window, lighting and performance generate a Gothic atmosphere. When the children are attacked in the woods by a groaning figure, his spindly hand appears like a claw before Scout's petrified stare. (Indeed, this scene recalls the opening scene of Charles Dickens' *Great Expectations*.) The style and execution of these scenes evokes horror movies such as *Frankenstein* (1931). In that film, a little girl is frightened by Frankenstein's Monster near a lake. What horror movies seek to do is to explore issues that are too controversial to be discussed in more mainstream genres such as melodrama, crime or soap operas. Horror movies use ghastly or monstrous images or effects as metaphors for real but 'difficult' problems such as rape, incest or homosexuality. In *To Kill a Mockingbird* Ewell's excessive behaviour with his daughter is channelled into his Gothic representation. To the film's middle class family audience, Ewell becomes a monster.

Because horrible gossip has surrounded the figure of Boo Radley, this gentle backward man has also become demonized. Boo's 'awful' reputation is carefully built up until the climactic moment when we actually see this quiet figure in Jem's room. The townsfolk don't understand so they have deployed metaphors that the film echoes with horror movie conventions. Like Cunningham, Bob Ewell is poor and feels less of a man for it. In an era when the Kennedy administration committed itself to conquering all social ills, Cunningham, Ewell and Boo Radley are seen as the victims of "cruel poverty and ignorance."

To Kill a Myth . . .

Big mainstream releases like *To Kill a Mockingbird* tend to embody easily understood and assimilated attitudes. After all, expensive to produce, they must appeal to a wide range of people if they are to turn a profit. Seeing the film from an early-21st-century perspective, what do you think of a white lawyer defending an African-American victim of racial hatred whilst keeping an African-American maid? How would an audience in America in 1962 have read this? How do you think contemporary African-Americans would have responded to that scene in which black people in the gallery rise in tribute to Gregory Peck's white lawyer defending their rights? How should we deal with the prospect of a little girl befriending a grown man with learning difficulties? Such questions invite us to ask why the film was made as it was and whether we have changed. Finally, how would you reconcile Atticus's philosophy with what you would see as you stepped out of an afternoon showing of *To Kill a Mockingbird* in a Mississippi picture theatre in 1962?

ROBERT BUTLER ON HARPER LEE'S RELIGIOUS VISION IN *TO KILL A MOCKINGBIRD*

Though less obviously than O'Connor or Walker, Lee also writes within a deep religious tradition. This tradition enabled her to endow *To Kill a Mockingbird* with a thematic depth, technical complexity, and cultural resonance that have helped to make it a remarkable achievement in modern American fiction. Although much discussion of the novel has focused on its sensationalistic, sometimes sentimentalized order action, the book's central meanings can be accessed most readily by exploring Lees religious vision, particularly her use of important concepts and symbols from Christian tradition. Her view of human life can be understood better in fundamental Christian terms than in political or sociological ones, with the motives and actions of her characters stemming more from mysterious spiritual drives than from psychological impulses reducible to secular analysis. In the final analysis, Lee is essentially a southern *religious* writer, one more concerned about sin and salvation than crime and punishment.

Perhaps the best way to begin probing the novel's religious vision is to analyze its epigraph, taken from Charles Lamb: "Lawyers, I suppose, were children once." This brief quotation suggests two worlds that the novel posits as quite distinct and oftentimes opposed to each other: (1) a rational, secular world of lawyers characterized by man-made laws intended to guarantee justice and order in society and (2) a universe of children characterized by instinctively perceived moral and spiritual realities. Whereas the book's outer narrative dramatizes the failure of secular law to live up to its promises, the book's inner narrative makes moral and spiritual affirmations transfiguring the external plot.

The outer social setting of *To Kill a Mockingbird* is portrayed as a grimly naturalistic place that crushes the human spirit and reduces to negative social conditioning the laws it has constructed to preserve its values and institutions. The "tired old town" (11) of Maycomb is an Alabama backwater deep in the throes of some of the worst years of the Great Depression. Inhabitants of Maycomb are hemmed in not only by its economic stagnation but also by customs fiercely enforced through informal gossip and formal laws of segregation. Everyone is victimized by such a rigidly constructed social world, from the effete snobs at the top of the social pyramid to the impoverished blacks who form its bottom layer. Anyone whom the town regards as different, such as Dolphus Raymond or Boo Radley, is crudely stereotyped and marginalized.

Maycomb, a town outwardly resembling Twain's Hadleyburg or Faulkner's Mottstown, has three crippling institutions: its schools, white churches, and courts. Each is dedicated to maintaining "Maycomb's ways" (36), social patterns rooted in ignorance, prejudice, and fear, Scout resents going to school because it wastes her time with meaningless routine, what she describes as "unrelieved boredom" (39), and takes her away from her real education consisting of her own reading and independent experience in the actual world. She is told she has to go to school because the law requires it, but she resents the fact that the "Good Citizenship" (39) the school preaches amounts to nothing more than conformity to a stagnant society. The town's white churches function in the same way. They are rigidly segregated and serve mainly to promote useless ladies' societies and conventional justifications for an unjust society.

The courthouse, located down the street from the schoolhouse and not far from the white church, also preserves the status quo rather than provide genuine law and order. It punishes innocent people such as Tom Robinson and fails to protect citizens from genuinely dangerous men like Bob Ewell. All three institutions uphold a "fake peace" (158) that dissolves midway through the novel when real evil erupts is the town.

In contrast to this outward environment is the redemptive world of children, one that Lee endows with moral innocence and innate spirituality. Scout expresses her acute awareness of the two worlds of the novel when she observes how "Aunt Alexandra fitted into the world of Maycomb like a hand into a glove, but never into the world of Jem and me" (142). Whereas her aunt tries to force her to accept a fixed role in a conventional society by becoming a "lady" (242), Scout doggedly persists in holding on to her status as a tomboy because she instinctively feels that the "ethical culture" (42) of children is superior to the hypocritical pieties of an adult society that endorses segregation and cruelly labels people such as Dolphus Raymond and Boo Radley. Like Huckleberry Finn, Holden Caulfield, and many other American child heroes, Scout prefers the company of children and childlike adults because she sees them as possessing an innate morality and spirituality. At times Atticus also sees children as moral touchstones. An attorney who is acutely aware of the limitations of the law and who has developed a "profound distaste for the practice of criminal law" (11) because he sees it as consistently failing to uphold real justice and moral order, Atticus is ethically inspired by his children. He knows they "'can spot an evasion quicker than adults'" (96) because their moral lights have not been darkened by a corrupt social system. He takes on the defense of Tom Robinson even though he is gravely pessimistic about the ability of southern law to preserve justice because he feels that he cannot "'face [his] children otherwise'" (97).

In the novel's climactic scene where Scout and Jem are threatened with death by Maycomb's most malevolent adult, Bob Ewell, the children are failed by both the law and the adults who are responsible for protecting them, as neither

Atticus, Calpurnia, Aunt Alexandra, nor Sheriff Heck Tate are present. But they are saved by the mysterious appearance of Boo Radley, who has the mind, heart, and spirit of a child. (The one time he speaks in the novel he whispers "in the voice of a child" [292].) It is significant that Lee presents Boo Radley and Bob Ewell in this scene—and throughout the novel—in theological rather than secular terms. Ewell's evil goes well beyond any of the socially induced corruption of Maycomb's other inhabitants and is presented as having what the American Puritans would call an innate depravity, an evil deriving from "congenital defects" (181) rather than environmental forces. Like Melville's Claggart[1] or Twain's Pap Finn, Ewell is regarded by even Atticus as irremediable, "'absolute trash'" (134). Boo, in sharp contrast, is endowed with an innate goodness that cannot be understood in any secular way. His difficult environment, including at-home incarceration for his entire adult life, should have made him the monster the town perceives him to be, but in fact he is a decent and courageous man. It is only children who can understand Boo: as they draw him out into the open in order to *see* him, they rightly perceive him as an innocent, even saintly, figure. They are struck by his goodness, generosity, and kindness, regarding him finally as a guardian angel of sorts who saves them from a man whose very name—"Ewell"—suggests "evil."

Boo is presented mysteriously throughout the novel, suggesting his status as a spiritual force. He appears and disappears almost magically, somehow knowing when he is needed to protect children from danger. . . .

Our final image of him bathed in "light from the livingroom windows" which "glistened on his forehead" (291) imbues him with a kind of radiance and luminescence one sees in characters like Dostoevsky's prince Myshkin. . . .

Although early critics faulted Lee's novel for straining verisimilitude by ascribing adult thoughts to a child narrator, it is important to remember that Scout tells her story in retrospect from the point of view of an adult who is able to "look back" on the novel's events when "enough years had gone by" (9) to understand them. She is no longer the traumatized child who witnesses the trial of Tom Robinson and barely escapes death when attacked by Bob Ewell. Although we do not know her precise age when she narrates the book, she has grown substantially and has acquired what she terms "a broad view" (9) of her experiences. This broad perspective, which Atticus and Miss Maudie have nurtured, teaches her about life in ways that her formal education failed to do. It enables her to understand that life is a complex mixture of good and evil and that the experience of pain can lead to healing and growth. . . .

In the short run, the evil observed by Scout and Jem simply stuns and disorients them. But as Scout thinks at the trial, "So many things had happened so fast I felt it would take years to sort them out" (220). By the time she has come to narrate the novel, she has indeed "sorted out" some of the novel's most disturbing events and has begun to see them in a fuller, more balanced way, understanding in a preliminary, inchoate way the Christian paradox that good can come out of evil and that our "falls" can be "fortunate" if we bring to them the wisdom and courage her father demonstrates throughout the novel. For this reason Jem is right when he observes that the events of the trial have made him like a "'caterpillar in a cocoon'" (228). At "nearly thirteen" (9), Jem is at the end of his childhood and, if he is able to perceive the events of the novel as Atticus sees them and Scout is beginning to see them, he will grow from his suffering.

The novel perhaps holds out hope for the South as it tries to understand its tragic past and move toward a better future. Miss Maudie may be right when she tells Jem that "' . . . we're making a step—it's just a baby-step, but it's a step'" (228). Even though the trial has resulted in the racial injustice that typifies the segregated South, there are signs of hope, since several of the town's leading citizens, including Atticus, Judge Taylor, and Sheriff Tate, are convinced of Tom's innocence and deplore the jury's verdict. And the fact that Maycomb reelects Atticus to the state legislature after the trial can be seen as a sign that the townspeople are beginning to accept his views. Although the novel was set during some of the darkest years of the Great Depression, it is very much a reflection of the time when it was written—a time when the civil rights movement, calling for a commitment to Christian values, was beginning to effect real change in the South.

Published in 1960, *To Kill a Mockingbird* is clearly centered in the faith in Christian community that was at the heart of the freedom movement in the late 1950s and early 1960s. Just as the Reverend Dr. Martin Luther King Jr. reminded Americans of Paul Tillich's warning that "sin is separation" (King 82) and called for renewed community in America founded upon the idea that "We are caught in an inescapable network of mutuality" (77), Lee uses her novel to argue that the physical differences separating us are not nearly as important as the spiritual qualities uniting us. . . .

The novel ends with Scout's own redemptive vision of a community held together with Christian love. Overcoming her initial terror and the disorientation brought on by Ewell's attack, she is calmed by Boo's gentleness, warmth, and radiant presence. When he asks her in a childlike whisper to take him "'home'" (292), she does so and returns to her own home with a renewed sense of its power and beauty. Deeply touched by her contact with Boo, she experiences her world as transfigured: "I turned to go home. Street lights winked down the street all the way to town. I had never seen our neighborhood from this angle. There were Miss Maudie's, Miss Stephanie's—there was our house, I could see the porch swing—Miss Rachel's house was beyond us, plainly visible. I could even see Mrs. Dubose's" (293). No longer seeing Maycomb as "a tired old town" (11) filled with strange eccentrics and afflicted with an ancient "disease" (97), Scout now perceives it from a new "angle" as it is illuminated by streetlights that "winked" and a rising sun that washes over everything with "Daylight" (293). Maycomb now becomes a "neighborhood" of integrally connected people. This new "angle" of perception allows her to experience Atticus's dictum that "'You never really understand a person until you consider things from his point of view . . . until you climb into his skin and walk around in it'" (36). And it beautifully reinforces her earlier conviction that "'. . . there's just one kind of folks. Folks'" (240). Adopting this notion of Christian interconnectedness, Scout now realizes that "Boo was our neighbor" (293) and that her world is filled with neighbors, not strangers. Her "longest journey" (267), which began when she and Jem returned from the Halloween party in pitch darkness, now concludes with her returning "home" (293) as she looks at her neighborhood in a fresh, revitalizing way, feeling securely placed in a world of flawed but loving people.

The novel concludes with an epiphany which blends Scout's new inward vision of Christian community with her outward experiences at home as her father reads to her while she falls asleep. The actual night fades as her "mind" creates a "Daylight" (293) vision of a busy community where neighbors converse, Miss Maudie tends her azaleas, and children scamper down the sidewalk to greet their father when he returns from work. Scout then imagines the main events of the novel as they pass from innocent summer play to more disturbing episodes of Atticus shooting the rabid dog and children stopping at the oak tree where Ewell's attack took place. The vision then turns to the summer of the trial with Atticus watching his children, powerless to prevent their "heart break" (294).

But the novel concludes in healing through love and deepened consciousness, not heartbreak. Children are finally protected by potent figures of love as Scout has finally found her "way home" (294). Atticus, who has earlier been identified as "a deep reader, a mighty deep reader" (179), eases her anxieties and enables her to sleep peacefully by helping her to "read" her own life so that she can ultimately "see" people and events from a Christian perspective. Such an outlook does not discount evil as an active force in the world, but it also reminds her that, in the long run, good triumphs over evil. After all, "'most people'" are "'real nice'" when "'you finally see them'" (295–96). This essentially Christian vision, like the oak tree Scout imagines in her dream, reveals that human life is cause not only for apprehension and puzzlement but also for love and faith.

Note

1. Robert Ryan's portrayal of Claggart in *Billy Build* is rivaled by James Anderson's depiction of Bob Ewell in *To Kill a Mockingbird*.

These actors convey an evil so malevolent and innate as not to be explainable in sociological or psychological terms.

Works Cited

Adams, Phoebe. "The Atlantic Bookshelf." Review of *To Kill a Mockingbird*, by Harper Lee. *Atlantic Monthly* 206 (August 1960): 98–99.

Chase, Richard. *The American Novel and Its Tradition*. Garden City, N.Y., Doubleday, 1957.

Twain, Mark. *Adventures of Huckleberry Finn*. 1884. New York: Norton. 1961.

Conrad, Joseph. *Heart of Darkness*. 1902. New York: Norton, 1963.

Hicks, Granville. "Three at the Outset." *Saturday Review* July 23. 1960: 15–16.

Ibsen, Henrik. *The Wild Duck*, trans. James Walter McFarlane. In *Modern Drama*, ed. Anthony Caputi. New York: Norton, 1966.

King, Rev. Dr. Martin Luther, Jr. *Why We Can't Wait*. New York: Mentor Books, 1964.

O'Connor, Flannery. *Mystery and Manners*. New York: Noonday, 1961.

Walker, Alice. *In Search of Our Mothers' Gardens*. San Diego: Harcourt Brace Jovanovich, 1983.

KATHRYN LEE SEIDEL ON SCOUT'S IDENTITY CHALLENGE AND EVOLUTION IN THE NOVEL

To Kill a Mockingbird, Harper Lee's enormously popular novel, paints a portrait of the young Jean Louise, or Scout as we know her, and her father, Atticus. The narrator recalls the story of herself as a child some thirty years earlier. The Jean Louise Finch who speaks as the narrator differs from the adult woman whom she also recollects. She is not a southern belle, she is not a bigot, she is not violent. She is not like Alexandra, Scout's aunt who wishes her to become a southern lady, nor has she grown up to be Mayella, the anti-belle, whose uncontrolled passions engender a series of violent acts against innocent people. Nor has she become a southern lady such as the bigoted Mrs. Merriweather, nor is she a member of a mob or married to one. She is wise; rational; aware of issues of gender, race, and caste; reverential of the innocence of children; and saddened by the tendency of individuals and society to urge children to commit the sins of their fathers.

How does Scout become Jean Louise Finch? How does she become neither the flower of southern belledom that Aunt Alexandra urges nor a woman still as impulsive and violent as she was when her name was Scout? A series of female role models and male friends allow her to test various versions of the adult she can become. Most influential in her development is her father, Atticus, who counters southern dicta for southern children with a philosophy of calm courage and rational strength. The novel sets up a counterpoint of the southern code of honor, with its entreaties to violent retribution and impulsive recourse to mob rule, with the philosophy of restraint and control embodied in the author's choice of the name of Scout's father, Atticus.

Atticus was the friend of the Roman philosopher Tullius Cicero, the statesman and lawyer known for his admiration for the Stoics' conceptualization of life, including the belief that people embody natural laws enabling control of passion, love of justice, and courage horn from reason. Lee's allusion to this school of thought is borne out in the novel's discourse between the dignity that Stoics accorded to the individual's role in society on one hand and the southern code of honor in which the individual's loss of face within the tribal group justifies acts of revenge and violence on the other. These precepts help Scout resist the influences pulling her into conventional southern womanhood by subverting her predilection towards violence, impulsivity, and prejudice. . . .

Scout has much to grapple with as a young girl attempting to grow up, not the least of which is her early rejection of "the conventional roles assigned to girls and women" (123), as Laura Fine writes. Because she is a southerner, and because southerners have conventional beliefs regarding their upper-class women, Scout's life story could have conformed to the hundreds of novels with southern belles in them. In these novels, the daughter of the aristocratic father, often a plantation owner during antebellum days or a lawyer in the postbellum

South, is typically portrayed as a motherless child with a close—sometimes an abnormally close—relationship with her father. . . . The absence of a strong and loving female parent in many such novels distorts the father–daughter relationship; the young girl practices her wiles on her father for her eventual days of courtship. The goal of this behavior is to attract a wealthy young man, preferably one whose family lands are adjacent and whose lineage is impeccable. Not having developed any inner qualities, she as an adult cannot let go of her narcissism and becomes a source of chaos in the lives of her family. . . .

Lee rejects this paradigm, but is fully aware of it as she writes. In this novel the person who is most like the southern belle is Mayella, whom Lee dissects with damning precision. In contrast, Lee examines how Scout as a southern girl can become fully human and not a Mayella or one of the many versions of southern women whom we meet in the novel. This may have been enough to make the novel interesting, but Lee moves beyond the examination of southern girlhood in this novel.

In fact, Scout's problem of identity in the novel is not that she is in danger of becoming any one of these versions of southern womanhood. Rather, her central problem is that she is in danger of becoming a southerner. Scout embodies all the faults of the Old South when we first meet her. She is prone to violence; she fights for apparently no reason other than her honor and her own amusement. She is an elitist. She labels people according to their social class, denigrates them, and justifies her mistreatment of them because of what she perceives to be their genetic tendency for inferior behavior. She uses racist language, for example, asking Atticus, "'Do you defend niggers . . . ?'" (82). She is prejudiced against all manner of persons, including African Americans and people of lower social classes. She believes in and is a practitioner of the code of honor rather than the rule of law: it is this code that leads her to punch her cousin when he insults her (92).

The novel is indeed a bildungsroman in which Scout must grow from innocence to maturity, but her innocence is sharply defined by tendencies which if developed could lead her to becoming the worst type of southerner with the worst prejudices and behaviors—a member of a mob, rather than a member of the good. She must learn empathy (36) and compromise (38) and, as her father says, to fight "'with [her] head,'" not her fists (84). She must learn to respect African Americans and people from the lower classes. As Eric Sundquist points out, *Mockingbird* is very much a novel of its time, informed as much by *Brown vs. Board of Education* as by the Depression era of its setting. Sundquist asserts that the dawn of desegregation in the South allows Lee to prepare southerners for a revisioning as moving away from traditional attitudes and becoming more wise, more tolerant (184). It is Scout who makes the journey that Lee is espousing, a journey from prejudice to tolerance, from ignorance to wisdom, from violence to self-control, from bigotry to empathy. from a code of honor to a code of law.

Scout likes to fight. Of the many altercations in the novel involving her, she practices on Walter Cunningham by "rubbing his nose in the dirt" (29). She beats up Dill twice to get his attention, "but it did no good," she tells us, as "he only grew closer to Jem" (48). She fights Walter Cunningham in the schoolyard as a matter of honor, such as she has begun to understand it, because she thinks that as a Cunningham, a member of a lower class, he deserves to be shown his place. Atticus says, "'I'm not worried about Jem keeping his head, but Scout'd just as soon jump on someone as look at him if her pride's at stake'" (96). In the code of honor, fights with people of lower classes are a way of asserting power and delivering justice; Scout interprets the code accurately and believes that inferior social status innately deserves some kind of punishment (Wyatt-Brown 162–63). . . . Contemporary psychologists such as Gayle Benham and Kaye Bultemeier who write on women and anger note that violence often results from the desire for "power in the interpersonal realm" (68). Deborah Cox writes in *Women's Anger: Clinical and Developmental Perspectives* how incidents of anger and violence can be an attempt to enhance self-esteem and self-identity; especially in children, violence externalizes a desire for power and the need to defend boundaries (192). The South is about boundaries—boundaries of space, boundaries of territory, boundaries of class, boundaries of caste—and Scout is, at age eight, attuned to these boundaries as if they are precious objects which she is determined to defend.

In fact, her explanation to her teacher for Walter Cunningham's having no lunch—and his declining to borrow money to buy some—is "'Miss Caroline, he's a Cunningham'" (26). Scout is so class-conscious that when Walter is invited to dinner, she refuses to be polite to him, explaining to Calpurnia, "'He ain't company, Cal, he's just a Cunningham—'" (31). If she is to become something other than a class-bound person whose worldview endorses violence and rudeness, Atticus must take measures. His methods differ entirely from what Scout associates with southern patriarchy, and she expects very little from him because at first she sees only his anti-patriarchal traits. He does not drive a dump truck; he wears glasses and "[doesn't] do anything" (97). Scout is embarrassed because "he never went hunting, he did not play poker or fish or drink or smoke. He sat in the livingroom and read" (98). To Scout, Atticus is a disappointment. Patiently he instructs her regarding realities that she at first does not want to face: "'You never really understand a person until you consider things from his point of view—, . . . until you climb into his skin and walk around in it'" (36).

As a parent, he also provides her with important appropriate affection. In much southern fiction, a father who desires to develop his daughter into a belle focuses on her personal appearance; compliments about her hair or her beauty, and touching her inappropriately, typify the father–daughter relationship in many novels about the southern belle. Instead, when Atticus and Scout are physically closest, he is always reading to her or teaching. . . . Atticus makes no reference to his wife physically; his admonition to Scout is that true courage is related to "'the way we conduct ourselves when the chips are down'" (113). He gives as an example Mrs. Dubose in her fight against addiction, which has nothing to do with violence, guns, mobs, or any kind of confrontation. Later he tells Scout, "'. . .

I wanted you to see what real courage is, instead of getting the idea that courage is a man with a gun in his hand. It's when you know you're licked before you begin but you begin anyway and you see it through no matter what'" (121).

The young Scout hears and barely understands, but Jean Louise, the adult narrator, is portraying Atticus as a new form of southerner. He is not the acquiescent gentleman of many southern novels such as Ashley Wilkes in *Gone with the Wind*, nor is he indulgent like Clare's father in *Uncle Tom's Cabin*, who chases her and pelts her with roses. Atticus has the qualities associated with manhood prized in the South but chooses not to use them. He is a southerner who is "'the deadest shot in Maycomb County'" (106) as Miss Maudie says, but he resorts to violence only when necessity presents itself, as the episode with the mad dog indicates. He is a person who respects the law, not the honor code, because "'in our courts all men are created equal'" (218) in the Jeffersonian sense, not equal in ability but equal in natural rights. He recognizes that the society in which he lives is not ideal: women cannot serve on juries (234), while African Americans such as Tom are treated badly. . . .

Cicero wrote that conduct toward oneself, one's wife, and one's children should be the same as one's conduct toward society (Harris 308). Atticus helps Scout see how race, caste, gender, and the prejudices of southerners are not part of natural law, whereas courage, empathy, and reason are, and that developing them is crucial to becoming a good human being. He says to Scout, "'Try fighting with your head for a change . . . it's a good one, even if it does resist learning'" (84).

Scout does learn, but in doing so she must accept or resist the other characters in the novel who represent myriad points of view which reinforce or contradict Atticus's teachings. Miss Maudie is a supporter of Atticus with attitudes that resemble those of the adult, Jean Louise. She respects Atticus because he does not have a double standard toward women and blacks. She does not believe that women are "'a sin by definition'" (52). When Mrs. Merriweather demeans African Americans, it is Miss Maudie who is brave enough to scorn her verbally. Aunt Alexandra defines southern ladyhood for Scout with admonitions to wear dresses, to learn to cook, to curb her tongue. Learning to be a lady, the narrator observes, "involved playing with small stoves, tea sets, and wearing the Add-a-Pearl necklace. . . . [F]urthermore, I should be a ray of sunshine in my father's lonely life" (89). Atticus supports Scout, telling her that "there were already enough sunbeams in the family and to go on about [her] business" (89). . . . At her worst, Alexandra wants to send away Calpurnia because she has introduced tolerant attitudes toward others by taking Scout to the African American church and has undercut Alexandra's code of gender identity by allowing her to wear overalls. Atticus supports Calpurnia, not his own sister, and refuses to dismiss her, saying that Calpurnia has "'been harder on them in some ways than a mother would have been . . . she's never let them get away with anything. . . . She tried to bring them up according to her lights, and Cal's lights are pretty good—and another thing, the children love her'" (147).

This African-American housekeeper is the novel's female parental figure for Scout. It is Calpurnia who teaches Scout to write, it is she who admonishes Scout to treat little Walter with respect at dinner, and it is she who along with Atticus provides love and affection to Scout. She tells Scout she misses her when she is at school (35). Scout tries to fight with her verbally: "Our battles were epic and one-sided. Calpurnia always won, mainly because Atticus always took her side" (12). Like a husband–wife team presenting a united front, Calpurnia treats Scout well and defends her father as her father defends Calpurnia. A major scene regarding her influence is the visit to the African-American church in which Scout encounters Lulu, a proto-black militant who is angry with Calpurnia, saying that the white children have their own church. Calpurnia retorts, "'It's the same God, ain't it?'" (129). Because she has a family and her own social group, Calpurnia is many steps away from the mammies of southern literature who exist only for the sake of the white family. . . .

The polar opposite of Scout in the novel is Mayella, who is the nearest person to the southern belle Scout could become. In many novels, the belle uses seduction on the wrong man, as do Temple Drake in Faulkner's *Sanctuary* and Jenny Blair in Ellen Glasgow's *The Sheltered Life*. Mayella is not a daughter of the upper class but otherwise has many of the standard belle traits. She is another young woman in the novel who has no mother. She is seductive, self-absorbed, and destructive. Unlike the belle, however, she is poor, is in the lowest social class, that is, "white trash," and has a violent father who rapes her. Mayella has little opportunity to become anything other than belligerent and pathetic. Her sad attempt to seduce Tom underscores the destructiveness of the belle gone wild. Her father is the opposite of Atticus; their carnal relationship has been continuous. According to Atticus's definition of it ("carnal knowledge of a female by force and without consent" [145]), Mayella has indeed been raped by her father, since he beats her if she does not comply. Her most successful relationship to date is a minute each day with the polite and pleasant Tom.

Mayella is the anti-Scout: she has no restraint, no understanding of the moral community in which she lives, no courage to control her anger and her impulses. . . .

Scout's insight regarding Mayella signals an important theme in the novel, that of the outsider who cannot join with society. The novel shows that without careful instruction by a loving parent, a girl such as Scout could become another Mayella, an outcast because of her destructiveness. Atticus's philosophical views instruct Scout along her path, and she begins to realize that other children, such as Boo and Dill, are not so fortunate. As Claudia Johnson contends, Scout must confront the outcasts of her town, just as the South must confront the grotesque reality of violent racism (*Threatening* 67–72). . . .

At the end of the novel the concept of a lady has been linked to natural politeness and respect. Scout has become brave, not reckless; courageous, not violent. She is a lady in the best sense. Her greeting to Boo—"'Hey, Boo'" (285)—is the moment of recognition when Bow is no longer an outcast, a gray ghost, but a person, reclaimed into the human community. It signals that Scout herself is no longer a romantic or southern racist, but a realist. She says to her father, "'Atticus, he was real nice

... '" (295), and he responds, "'Most people are ... when you finally see them'" (296). The goal of the Stoic philosopher was to see people as they are, which is defined as naturally good. Her saying "'Hey, Boo'" is the moral equivalent of Huckleberry Finn's statement "All right, then, I'll *go* to hell" when he finally comes to see Jim as he is, a friend and protector, and not as a marginalized or inferior person. Scout has learned that white trash mobs are still people, that Tom Robinson is a person, that Mayella is lonely, that Boo is to be treated as the delicate creature that he is. If she had become a southerner, imbued with the code of honor, these would all be invisible to her. Indeed, they become real precisely because she can now see them. . . .

Scout has made the journey from an incipient southern racist, belle, or bigot to a courageous, honest, rational member of the human community. Her father has helped elicit her natural goodness while encouraging her to develop courage with restraint and dignity with compassion. At age eight, Scout Finch is ready to become the narrator whom we meet thirty years later.

JACQUELINE TAVERNIER-COURBIN ON THE USE OF HUMOR IN THE TRIAL

Much like beauty, humor is in the eye—or the mind—of the beholder: as Charles Baudelaire wrote in *De l'essence du rire*: "Le comique, la puissance du rire est dans le rieur et nullement dans l'objet du rire" [The comical, the power of laughter is in the one who laughs and not in the object of laughter] (541). Although Scout is not trying to be funny, her point of view—at once naïve, candid, and clear-sighted—is a source of humor in much of the novel. Indeed what one laughs at tells much about who one is, and some readers will certainly perceive humor in the unexpectedness of her puns, similes, and metaphors; in the childishness of some of her comments that point out the discrepancies between childhood and adulthood; in the appropriateness of some of her observations that highlight the gulf between things as they should be and as they are (providing in particular a sharp satire of the educational system); and in her descriptions of small-town life in Alabama. Her need for acceptance, her growing-up trials, and her resistance to behaving like a girl are also pervaded with humor as well as dramatic irony. Black humor, however, takes over during the trial of Tom Robinson and arises largely from Atticus's ability to reveal what really happened during the alleged rape. Through his cross-examination of the Ewells, his exposure of their lies, their deep ignorance and stupidity, one is able to laugh at them, even if not at the monstrosity of their crime, and to view them as both evil and pitiful. Thus what could be an unbearably painful story is relieved by a deep-seated humor that fosters perspective and a profound pity for, and eventual acceptance of, the human condition. As Harper Lee wished it to be, her book is not only a bitter satire of crowd psychology and racism but also a plea for understanding and an attempt to give a sense of proportion to life in the South.[1]

Taken in its most general sense as a generic term for everything that appeals to man's disposition toward comic laughter, humor includes in particular wit, parody, irony, and satire—the expressions of a mind-set that tends toward life, survival, and enjoyment in the face of pain, death, and injustice. Clearly, laughter in itself is not synonymous with humor, nor is it a sufficient yardstick by which to measure humor: after all, laughter can arise from experiences unrelated to humor, such as tickling, nervousness, high spirit, play, or make-believe. Similarly pleasure and humor are not the same thing, but both pleasure and laughter, either inward or outward, are end results of the humor experience, although not its source. In fact, according to Nietzsche, man alone suffers so excruciatingly in the world that he was compelled to invent laughter, thus creating pleasure out of displeasure. Most writers agree with Nietzsche and see humor as arising out of man's sadness and despair. Indeed, for Mark Twain, "Everything human is pathetic. The secret source of Humor itself is not joy but sorrow. . . . There are countless theories that try to define humor, but whether these theories be specifically identified with superiority, incongruity, ambivalence, release and relief, configuration, or psychoanalysis, almost all forms of humor involve three elements: surprise, acceptance, and insight. The surprise usually arises out of the perception of incongruity— the perception of disjointed, ill-suited pairings of ideas or situations. The acceptance, or reconciliation, arises when the unrelated elements fall into place. This phenomenon leads to a new and unexpected revelation or insight. The three-part sequence collectively creates amusement. . . .

The trial of Tom Robinson introduces a different type of humor that does not arise from Scout's and Jem's behavior and remarks. It is a type of humor perhaps best described as "a sickeningly comic aspect of an unfunny situation" (162), if one may borrow Scout's comment on the night a mob goes to the jail to lynch Tom. When Atticus tells the would-be lynchers that Tom is asleep, they start talking in near-whispers, considerate enough not to wake him when they would hang him. Conditioned reflexes can override logical action even in the direst situations. This is indeed black humor, an attempt, as Roland Wallace puts it, to "face the void without flinching," to "endure the absurd, and, by viewing life from a comic perspective, . . . enjoy the endurance" (qtd. in Pratt 189). According to Patrick O'Neil, black humorists "all share the same detachment, the same irony, . . . the same undercutting of all systems, . . . and above all . . . one central characteristic: a refusal to treat what one might regard as tragic materials tragically . . ." (O'Neil 65). Of course, it is difficult not to think of Samuel Beckett's definition in *Watt* of the bitter laugh that "laughs at that which is not good"; the hollow laugh that laughs "at that which is not true"; and the mirthless laugh, the laugh of laughs, that laughs "at that which is unhappy" (47). Black humor partakes of all three forms of laughter, but perhaps especially the last form, since it tends to encompass all.

Much of the humor of the trial arises from the cross-examination of the Ewells by Atticus. Central to its humor are the discrepancies between their sworn statements and the obvious impossibility of their claims, and between the ideal concept of justice and its often dismal practice. It is indeed as "unfunny" a situation as can be. A black man, Tom Robinson, is fighting for his life, accused of rape and battery of a white woman. What is even less funny is the fact that, although he is clearly innocent, his condemnation is a foregone conclusion merely because he is black (albeit respectable, honest, hardworking, and a loving family man) and the woman is white (even though she and her family are shiftless, ignorant, and contemptible). Nevertheless, it is impossible not to laugh at the enormity of their arrogance as Bob Ewell complains of how the blacks living near him are "'devaluin' [his] property'" (186): the blacks live in neat and snug cabins, with delicious smells wafting out, while the Ewells live at the dump in a shack made of planks and corrugated iron and roofed by "tin cans hammered flat" (181). What is even more humorously sickening is the fact that he has a point, as evidenced by the outcome of the trial. Personal qualities do not count; only skin color does.

The impossibility of Mayella's accusation is obvious and epitomized by Atticus's simple question: "'How?'" (198). Indeed, how could a one-armed man choke, beat, and rape a strong girl accustomed to strenuous labor who is supposedly fighting him off "'tooth and nail'" (192)? It is Atticus's achievement to make the ludicrousness of their claim obvious to everyone, and it is the rueful irony of the story that Tom will still be condemned to death when anyone with a molecule of honesty or common sense knows him to be innocent. The whole abstract concept of justice has been turned on its head and into a sad joke. Even worse, much of the community resents Atticus's defending Tom because it makes them face up to their willingness to kill him simply because he is black. Awful as the Ewells are, there are moments of humor that give the reader some insight into their miserable existence and defective emotional lives. There is, for instance, a certain amount of black humor when Atticus asks Bob Ewell whether he ran for a doctor to take care of Mayella after she was supposedly assaulted by Tom. Clearly, Ewell's lack of understanding of the need for such action speaks volumes (186–87). Of course, we know that Tom never raped Mayella, and that it is Bob Ewell who beat her up when he found her with Tom. But had she really been attacked by Tom, it is clear that Ewell still would not have been concerned with her physical or psychological welfare and certainly not enough to spend five dollars for a doctor. Clearly none of his children's lives is worth a doctor's visit, but a slight to his poor-white dignity is worth an innocent black man's death.

The ignorance of both Ewells is paradoxically matched by their cunning. When Bob Ewell is proven by Atticus to be left-handed, he is angry because he feels insulted but does not realize that only a left-handed man could have punched Mayella's right eye, which clearly exonerates Tom of having hit her. Amusingly, too, Ewell no more understands the meaning of the word "ambidextrous" (189) than Jem understands "caricature" (75). Taking the word as another insult and vehemently denying being ambidextrous, he is still cunning enough to feel that something is wrong and claims that he "'can use one hand [as] good as the other'" (189). Mayella, too, is cunning enough to try to get the judge and jury to feel sorry for her by objecting to being made fun of, as she feels her father was. The irony is, of course, that while both Ewells unwittingly do a great job of ridiculing themselves, no one is making fun of them—with the exception of the judge with his facial expression when looking at Bob Ewell during his testimony "as if he were some fragrant gardenia in full bloom on the witness stand" (188–89). Feeling that being identified as left-handed is an insult and that being called "Ma'am" or "Miss" is being mocked (193), Mayella paradoxically evokes pity by revealing what a sad and stunted life she has led—not quite what she intended to achieve. Aiming to project a picture of raped innocence, she instead projects a picture of duplicitous ignorance and inarticulate human misery. Clearly her life has been one of sordid poverty, devoid of even the most casual routine courtesy, of any form of friendship or human warmth, and dominated by a drunken and abusive father. It is thus bitterly ironic that she should hate and destroy the one person who showed her kindness, illustrating the paradoxical truth that no good deed ever goes unpunished. The contrast between the psychological logic of such behavior—"'destroy[ing] the evidence of her offense'"

(216)—and the teachings of morality, according to which good deeds are rewarded, are at the root of the humor and emphasize the need for a heaven where such things can be righted. But then, of course, there is no need for humor in heaven. . . .

The title of the novel itself involves humor, either more subtle than the rest of the novel's or perhaps unwitting on Lee's part, as suggested by the apparently serious explanation she provides: it's a sin to kill a mockingbird because "'they don't eat up people's gardens, don't nest in corncribs, they don't do one thing but sing their hearts out for us'" (98). From this as well as the obvious use of the mockingbird as a metaphor for Tom Robinson (254) and later Boo Radley (291), one sees the mockingbird as a helpless and peaceful songbird—which is quite inaccurate. Mockingbirds are small birds, with a wingspan of no more than ten to fifteen inches, but they are very aggressive, attacking other birds, even humans, and their own reflection. They are known as "bullies" among birds because they will chase other birds from the feeders and even their nests, as they want the best nesting places for themselves. They are also many-tongued mimics, able to reproduce the songs of other birds as well as other sounds. Thus the clear identification of the mockingbird with the two fairly helpless victims of the novel appears paradoxical. Indeed, Boo Radley's nature is no more aggressive than Tom Robinson's, although he develops teeth and claws at the end of the story to save the children.

A number of critics have discussed the novel's title, and while Calvin Woodard offers the most thorough examination of its relevance to the novel, he nevertheless does not take into account the belligerence of the little bird. Instead, he views the mockingbird largely as a symbol of tolerance because it identifies with, listens to, and learns from others; he sees it only as less than virtuous because it conforms too much to the will of others. This interpretation certainly does correspond with Lee's plea for tolerance but has little to do with humor. However, if one takes into account the mockingbird's aggressiveness, it then can become a symbol of hypocrisy rather than tolerance— pretending to be what it is not. Its emulating the songs of other birds would then link the mockingbird more closely to the "sickness" of intolerance and racism pervading the southern states, to the hypocrisy of the legal system merely going through the pretense of dispensing justice, and the mendacity of the missionary circle voicing Christian beliefs but contradicting them in action. Indeed, while the mockingbird is not the official state bird of Alabama, it is the state bird of five southern states and is generally seen as symbolizing the South.

Its very name evocatively including the word "mocking" (imitating, but also ridiculing through imitation, and expressing scorn), the mockingbird could also symbolize the satirist revealing the ugly underbelly of the South through humor. Laughter kills by exposing the gangrene under the beautiful surface but also by demeaning it; one can hardly allow oneself to be controlled by what one is able to laugh at. Thus those who laugh—i.e., those who are not taken in by pretenses but debunk the system and accepted norms—are not always popular with the powers that be, as the fate of many a satirist has witnessed throughout the centuries. Intolerance and fanaticism kill the "mockingbirds." However, satires and satirists have often been very popular with the reading public and have on occasion been known to be the instruments of change. This is the case with *To Kill a Mockingbird*. Thanks in large part to her skillful handling of humor, Harper Lee has created in her popular, unpretentious novel a still-powerful instrument for raising the level of consciousness about the effects of racism in the South.

Note
1. See, for example, Lee's statements in her 1963 interview with Bob Ellison.

Works by Harper Lee

To Kill a Mockingbird, 1960.

"Love—In Other Words" (magazine article), 1961.

"Christmas to Me" (magazine article), 1961.

"When Children Discover America" (magazine article), 1965.

"High Romance and Adventure," 1985.

Annotated Bibliography

Adams, Phoebe. "Summer Reading." *Atlantic Monthly:* August 26, 1960, pp. 98–99.

This is an oft-quoted, though brief review, in which Phoebe Adams dismisses *To Kill a Mockingbird* as a typical summer reading novel—pleasant and undemanding.

Barge, R. Mason. "Fictional Characters, Fictional Ethics." *Legal Times:* March 9, 1992.

One of the most heated responses to Monroe Freedman's article "Atticus Finch, Esq., R.I.P.," in which the author argues that Freedman is not only unrealistic in his politically conscious expectations, he unfairly judges Finch by contemporary standards.

Bloom, Harold, ed. *To Kill a Mockingbird*, new edition. Modern Critical Interpretations series. Chelsea House Publishers: New York, 2006.

A compendium of full-length essays on *To Kill a Mockingbird*, notably from R. A. Dave, Claudia Durst Johnson, and Fred Erisman.

Carter, Dan T. *Scottsboro: A Tragedy of the American South.* Baton Rouge: Louisiana State University, 1969.

A lucid account of the 1931 trial of nine black men that allegedly is one of the influences behind the trial of Tom Robinson. It also offers a detailed description of the atmosphere in Alabama around that time.

Crespino, Joseph. "The Strange Career of Atticus Finch." *Southern Cultures* 6, no. 2, 2000: 9.

Crespino discusses the liberalism of Atticus Finch as the driving force behind the morality in *To Kill a Mockingbird*.

Dave, R.A. "*To Kill a Mockingbird*: Harper Lee's Tragic Vision." *Indian Studies in American Fiction.* Calcutta: The Macmillan Company of India Limited, 1974: 311–323.

Dave discusses the elements of Greek tragedy in *To Kill a Mockingbird*, focusing on such topics as the battle between good and evil, tragic heroes, and the unity of place and action.

Erisman, Fred. "The Romantic Regionalism of Harper Lee." *Alabama Review* 26, no. 2, 1973: 126–136.

Erisman asserts that Harper Lee presents a dual view of the South—New and Old—in *To Kill a Mockingbird*, and that the South can no longer stand as a separate entity from the rest of the country.

Fisher, Jerilyn and Ellen S. Silber, eds. *Women in Literature: Reading through the Lens of Gender*. Westport, Conn., and London: Greenwood Press, 2003.

This study consists of 96 short essays, each dealing with a female character or characters or the absence of female characters in the most commonly read novels and short stories in world literature. The essay on *To Kill A Mockingbird* focuses on societal influences on the novel's narrator as she grows from young child to young woman.

Ford, Nick Aaron. "Battle of the Books: A Critical Survey of Significant Books by and about Negroes Published in 1960." *Phylon* 22, no. 2, 1961: 122–123.

Ford discusses the role of African Americans in *To Kill a Mockingbird*, asserting that Lee portrayed them in an honest, nonstereotypical way.

Freedman, Monroe. "Atticus Finch—Right and Wrong." *Alabama Law Review* 45, no. 2, 1994: 473–482.

Freedman discusses the moral education of Scout—especially how she must learn to incorporate the lessons of character from her father with the lessons of the prudence traditionally associated with her gender.

———. "Atticus Finch, Esq., R.I.P." *Legal Times*: February 24, 1992: 20.

In a controversial piece, Freedman argues that Atticus Finch is not a good role model for lawyers.

———. "Finch: The Lawyer Mythologized." *Legal Times:* May 18, 1992: 25.

Freedman responds to the controversy that he provoked with his article "Atticus Finch, Esq., R.I.P."

Going, William T. "Store and Mockingbird: Two Pulitzer Novels about Alabama." Tuscaloosa: University of Alabama Press: *Essays on Alabama Literature*, 1975: 9–31.

Going compares and contrasts T.S. Stribling's *The Store*, which is set in Florence, Alabama, with Lee's *To Kill a Mockingbird*.

Hovet, Theodore, and Grace-Ann Hovet. "'Fine Fancy Gentlemen'" and "'Yappy Folk'": Contending Voices in *To Kill a Mockingbird*. *Southern Quarterly* 40, no. 1, 2001: 67–78.

The Hovets demonstrate how issues of class and gender factor in the escalation of prejudice and racism in *To Kill a Mockingbird*.

Johnson, Claudia Durst. *"To Kill A Mockingbird": Threatening Boundaries*. New York: Twayne Publishers, 1994.

As widely read as *To Kill A Mockingbird* has been over the years since its publication in 1960, few literary scholars have taken much notice. Of the few who have, Claudia Durst Johnson is the best known and most frequently cited. This book-length study includes, in the first half, both biographical and chronological information about the author, a thoughtful discussion of racial tensions particular to the time and place of the novel, and a history of the critical and popular reception of the book. In the second half of the book, the author offers insights about the literary aspects of Lee's writing and commentary on the unfolding plot and issues raised by the aftermath of the trial. A substantial bibliography includes reviews and background reading about the racial climate, similar trials, lynchings, and the tension between acceptable behavior from a legal standpoint and that of the prevailing social codes. Johnson's study of Harper Lee's novel is an excellent resource for students.

———. *Understanding* To Kill a Mockingbird: *A Student Casebook to Issues, Sources and Historical Documents*. Westport, CT: Greenwood, 1994.

A highly useful and fascinating assembly of sources, the casebook includes interviews with southern women who grew up around the same time as Scout, transcripts from the Scottsboro trials, quotations from writers such as Faulkner about the plight of the "white trash," and detailed bibliographies throughout.

Johnson, Claudia. "Without Tradition and Within Reason: Judge Horton and Atticus Finch in Court." *Alabama Law Review* 45, no. 2, 1994: 483–510.

Johnson compares Atticus Finch with the real-life Judge Horton, who placed his position in jeopardy when he overturned the guilty verdicts at the Scottsboro trials and ordered a retrial.

Lemay, Harding. "Children Play; Adults Betray." *The New York Herald Tribune Book Review*. July 10, 1960: 5.

Lemay discusses the interweaving of childhood recollections with the harsher theme of racism in *Mockingbird*.

O'Neill, Terry, ed. *Readings on "To Kill A Mockingbird."* San Diego, California: Greenhaven Press, Inc., 2000.

This study of *To Kill A Mockingbird* is similar in focus and intended readership to the Johnson study cited previously in this section but takes advantage of some more recently published commentary on Harper Lee and the novel. The editor laments the relative paucity of scholarly attention to the novel and praises Johnson for her contributions. *Readings* is organized into four sections—the critical reception, literary techniques, social issues, and a close look at the character of Atticus Finch. A short essay discussing the plot, themes, and characters is also included as well as a brief chronology of Harper Lee's life.

Petry, Alice Hall, ed. *On Harper Lee: Essays and Reflections*. Knoxville, The University of Tennessee Press, 2007.

This collection of essays begins with a foreword by William T. Going, a scholar of southern literature who has been praising and promoting Harper Lee and her novel since it was first published. The essays are written specifically for this study and thus represent the most recent serious commentary on the novel published in book form.

Shakelford, Dean. "The Female Voice in *To Kill a Mockingbird*: Narrative Strategies in Film and Novel." *Mississippi Quarterly* 50, no. 1, 1996–1997.

Shakelford discusses the importance of the female voice and gender roles in *To Kill a Mockingbird*.

Shields, Charles. J. *Mockingbird: A Portrait of Harper Lee*. New York: Henry Holt and Company, 2006.

The author explains in his introduction that the singular and perennial popularity of Harper Lee's novel makes it imperative that—despite Lee's aversion to publicity—readers have some notion of who she was. According to Shields, Harper was not involved in producing his book. Without Lee's cooperation, the author had to rely on oral and written communications with everyone he could find who had had some kind of relationship with her; he secured more than 600 contacts to form the basis of his study.

Stuckey, W. J. *The Pulitzer Prize Novels: A Critical Backward Look*. Norman: University of Oklahoma Press, 1966.

In a section his book, Stuckey addresses the major defects in *To Kill a Mockingbird*, focusing on the discrepancies between the double plot.

Woodard, Calvin. "Listening to the Mockingbird." *Alabama Law Review* 45, no. 2, 1994: 563–584.

Woodard circumnavigates the obvious issue of the role of justice in the novel to attack what is considered the provenance of literary academics—that of symbolism, particularly that of the mockingbird and its relationship to the South.

Contributors

Harold Bloom is Sterling Professor of the Humanities at Yale University. Educated at Cornell and Yale universities, he is the author of more than 30 books, including *Shelley's Mythmaking* (1959), *The Visionary Company* (1961), *Blake's Apocalypse* (1963), *Yeats* (1970), *The Anxiety of Influence* (1973), *A Map of Misreading* (1975), *Kabbalah and Criticism* (1975), *Agon: Toward a Theory of Revisionism* (1982), *The American Religion* (1992), *The Western Canon* (1994), *Omens of Millennium: The Gnosis of Angels, Dreams, and Resurrection* (1996), *Shakespeare: The Invention of the Human* (1998), *How to Read and Why* (2000), *Genius: A Mosaic of One Hundred Exemplary Creative Minds* (2002), *Hamlet: Poem Unlimited* (2003), *Where Shall Wisdom Be Found?* (2004), and *Jesus and Yahweh: The Names Divine* (2005). In addition, he is the author of hundreds of articles, reviews, and editorial introductions. In 1999, Professor Bloom received the American Academy of Arts and Letters' Gold Medal for Criticism. He has also received the International Prize of Catalonia, the Alfonso Reyes Prize of Mexico, and the Hans Christian Andersen Bicentennial Prize of Denmark.

Patrick Chura is a professor in the English department at the University of Akron; he specializes in nineteenth- and twentieth-century literature. He is the author of *Vital Contact: Downclassing Journeys in American Literature from Herman Melville to Richard Wright*. Currently he is teaching American studies in Lithuania on a Fulbright Scholars Program grant.

Laurie Champion teaches in the English and comparative literature department at the Imperial Valley Campus of San Diego State University.

Isaac Saney is associate director of the Transition Year Program at Henson College of Dalhousie University. He is also a part-time faculty member in the International

Development Studies program at St. Mary's University in Halifax, Nova Scotia. Saney is a member of the Black Community Advocates Association of Nova Scotia.

Michele S. Ware teaches English and American literature at North Carolina Central University. In addition to her work on Harper Lee, she has focused on Edith Wharton, the American short story, and American women's political poetry.

Richard Armstrong has been a frequent contributor to *The Film Journal*.

Robert Butler teaches American, African-American, and modern literature at Canisius College in Buffalo, New York. He is also the director of the All-College Honors Program at the college. His other work includes *The Emergence of a New Black Hero* (1991), *The Critical Response to Richard Wright* (1995), *Contemporary African American Fiction: The Open Journey* (1998), and *The Critical Response to Ralph Ellison* (2000).

Kathryn Lee Seidel teaches English and is the dean of the College of Arts and Sciences at the University of Central Florida in Orlando. In addition to her work on *To Kill A Mockingbird*, she is the author of *The Southern Belle in the American Novel* (1985) and co-editor of *Zora in Florida* (1991). She has contributed many essays to journals.

Jacqueline Tavernier-Courbin is professor emerita of English at the University of Ottawa, Canada. For many years she was the editor of *Thalia: Studies in Literary Humor*. She devoted much of her career to the subject of literary humor and was considered a specialist in southern humor. Her published works include *Critical Essays on Jack London* (1983), *Ernest Hemingway's A Moveable Feast: The Making of a Myth* (1991), and *"The Call of the Wild": A Naturalistic Romance* (1994).

Acknowledgments

Patrick Chura, from "Prolepsis and Anachronism: Emmett Till and the Historicity of *To Kill a Mockingbird*." *Southern Literary Journal*, vol. 32, no. 2 (Spring 2000): 1–26. Copyright © 2000 by *Southern Literary Journal*.

Laurie Champion, from "Lee's *To Kill a Mockingbird*." *The Explicator*, vol. 61, no. 4 (Summer 2003): 234–36. Copyright © 2003 by *The Explicator*. Reprinted by permission of Heldref Publications, www.heldref.org

Isaac Saney, from "The Case Against *To Kill a Mockingbird*." *Race & Class*, vol. 45(1): 99–110. Copyright © 2003 Institute of Race Relations.

Michele S. Ware, from "'Just a Lady': Gender and Power in Harper Lee's *To Kill a Mockingbird* (1960)" in *Women in Literature: Reading Through the Lens of Gender*, edited by Jerilyn Fisher and Ellen S. Silber, pp. 286–88. Copyright © 2003 by Jerilyn Fisher and Ellen S. Silber. Reproduced with permission of ABC-CLIO, LLC.

Richard Armstrong, from "On *To Kill a Mockingbird*." *The Film Journal*, issue 11, unpaginated. Copyright © 2002–05, *The Film Journal*.

Robert Butler, from "The Religious Vision of *To Kill a Mockingbird*" in *On Harper Lee: Essays and Reflections*, edited by Alice Hall Petry, pp. 122–24, 129–33. Copyright © 2007 by the University of Tennessee Press/Knoxville.

Kathryn Lee Seidel, from "Growing Up Southern: Resisting the Code for Southerners in *To Kill a Mockingbird*" in *On Harper Lee: Essays and Reflections*, edited by Alice Hall Petry, pp. 79–88, 90. Copyright © 2007 by the University of Tennessee Press/Knoxville.

Jacqueline Tavernier-Courbin, from "Humor and Humanity" in *On Harper Lee: Essays and Reflections*, edited by Alice Hall Petry, pp. 42–43, 54–56, 58–59. Copyright © 2007 by the University of Tennessee Press/Knoxville.

Index

Characters in the novel are indexed by first name.